Send In The Clowns

Also by the same author

Weardale Days 'Up the Square'
Up The Square
The Day Trip
Tell Laura I Love Her
Turned Out Nice Again

A L Craig

Send In The Clowns

❀
Naylor Publishing

Published in Great Britain by
Naylor Publishing

ISBN 0-9538533-4-9
Printed and bound in Great Britain by
Resource Print Solutions – 0113 2058304

Chapter 1

The Phoenix Public House, Stanhope Co. Durham
10 May 2003

Whistling cheerily, John Craig unbolted the back door of his public house. He shuddered as a bracing breeze cut through him. The Saturday began here, he reflected. At fifty-nine and maybe a stone overweight, the balding publican grabbed with both hands any opportunity of a days outing with 'the lads.' Shackled to a public house twenty-four hours a day, he needed to get away now and again, if only to keep his sanity.

'Aboot ruddy time, I've been here ages! It's nearly five past ten man! If there's one thing ar canna stand, it's unpunctuality. You definitely said you'd be oppening up at ten o'clock sharp,' bemoaned the cantankerous Roy Osborne.

'Dear me, hold the front page, I'm a couple o' minutes late,' sighed the landlord.

'Well, that's ye all ower, tekking yer best customers fer granted,' said Roy, barging past John as if he were invisible in his haste to get to the bar.

'And good morning to you too,' said John, shaking his head.

'Ha way man, an' pull us a pint o' lager, ar's gagging. Me mouth's as dry as a nurse's pay packet. Oh, an' by the way, what

1

did yer spike the beer wi' last night? Apart from the usual gallons o' watter like. Ar feel as rough as a bear's arse this morning.'

'If there's summat wrong wi' your constitution, it's got nowt to do with my prize ales bonny lad. Yer'll 'ave been at that Chinese tek away again after yer left 'ere last night. Ar'll put me life on it. If you will eat that oriental muck, ar've nee sympathy with you whatsoever. Yer deserve all yer get.'

'Yer a hard man John Craig. Come to think of it, I might have partook of a Ruby Murray on my homeward journey . . . '

'You might have? Were yer that blathered?'

'Alright . . . I did 'ave a ruby - okay? Mind, there's nowt new in that of a Friday night. Most of the lads enjoy their weekly arse burner. I must admit though . . . it went through me like a dose of Andrew's Liver Salts first thing this morning. Ar kid ye not, I could shite through a Polo Mint wi' out touching the sides. Ar tell yer what John, yer divent dare fart in bed after a mucky curry. It's touch an' go whether it'd follow through or not.'

'Bah, you've a wonderful turn o' phrase, ar'll give you that much Royston. If them tek aways are as bad as you mek out, an' listening to ye lot every weekend going on aboot whether the chicken curry is actually cat or rat meat, why the hell do yer bother? It beats me. Get yer sens fish an' chips or summat else less gut wrenching,' suggested the landlord as he filled a pint glass with lager and passed it to a very thirsty Roy, noticing as he did, that if Roy's tongue hung out any further it would be touching the bar.

'Whey, it's tradition isn't it?' pointed out Roy.

'Is it? News to me, that one.'

'Course it is,' he insisted. 'Ar divent nar, ye old uns know nothing. Every Friday night me an' the lads always meet up here in your establishment, though ar divent nar why . . . '

'Hey, watch it laddie!'

Roy carried on regardless, 'We drink ten pints o' dish watter - what you call lager, an' then it's a trip to the chinky.' Roy chuckled. 'It's always a canny laugh in there mind after a few bevvies. Most weeks John Bickers, you nar, the local piss-head an' pill-popper.'

'Aye, tell me aboot him,' chuntered the landlord. 'Spewing up all ower my toilets. He's barred from these premises for life - which won't be long in his case, cos he doesn't give a toss. I warned him aboot his behaviour but he took no heed. It's watter off a duck's back man. I don't think fer a minute a single word I said registered in his pickled heed.'

'Anyway, where was I before I was rudely interrupted?' said Roy sarcastically.

'Pardon me for living.'

'Aye, that's it,' continued Roy. 'John Bickers'll stagger through the chinky door, stinking like a cesspit an' a brewery all rolled into one. He'll stand there swaying from side to side trying his best to focus on that vast menu up on the wall. After staring at it for ten minutes he'll suddenly pipe up in his usual loud slurred voice, "Ar'll 'ave gravy an' chips . . . hic . . . Gunga Din. Pronto!"'

'Gunga Din?' remarked John. 'What's he got to do wi' owt? He's not Chinese.'

'Yeah, I know, but nobody puts John right cos it's like talking to a brick wall at the best of times, never mind when he's paralytic.'

'Just as a matter of interest, how old will he be?'

'Now yer asking,' pondered Roy, stroking his chin. 'Thirty-seven or eight maybe. Summat like that.'

'It'll be a miracle if he sees forty then.'

'Aye, yer probably right. Ar must say one thing in his defence though.'

'Oh aye, an' what's that like?'

'Whey, he's harmless enough, but drink or no drink, I've never seen him turn violent. A nuisance maybe, but never violent. Ar feel sorry seeing a zombified bloke staggering aboot all the time.'

'Listen to pot calling kettle black.'

'How d'yer mean like?' objected Roy.

'Whey, he's no different to you an the lads every weekend, pissed as farts.'

'Aye, yer not wrong there,' conceded Roy with a wry smile. 'Ar've seen us in some canny states.'

'That's an understatement bonny lad.'

'Yer not complaining are yer? Brass you tek off us!'

3

'No, far from it. You keep drinking Roy lad. The more you sup, the better.'

'I never gan ower the top during the week though, do I John? Well - very rarely. I'd never get up fer work man.'

John left the confines of the bar to give a quick inspection of the games room. It wouldn't be for the first time if he came across the odd glass that the morning cleaner had over-looked. She was a grand lass was Jean, but a bit absent-minded. He passed the ornate coat stand in the hallway, glancing at the tatty PVC raincoat that had been hanging there for a month now. He'd give it another week and if it still wasn't claimed he'd bin it. If it had been left to his wife Gladys, she'd have got rid after a week. In her opinion it wasn't fit for wear and was making the place look untidy. Satisfied with the glass free games room, John returned to the lounge bar. Following the sound of footsteps on the stairs, his wife Gladys breezed through the living quarter door, a can of furniture polish in one hand, a spotless yellow duster in the other. She was a slim woman without an ounce of excess weight on her, due to the fact she was always darting about. John referred to her as Whirlwind Gladys and would often wind her up complaining about the draught she generated while whizzing round the bar with her duster, which was totally unnecessary when they had a daily cleaner, but Gladys would never change the habit of a lifetime. John had long since stopped chastising her about what he considered obsessional cleaning. She had countered this by saying she would cease the cleaning when he stopped his gambling on the horses. At fifty-seven Gladys had a lovely mop of jet-black hair with barely a trace of grey, which she always maintained was a minor miracle having been married to John for nearly thirty-five years. Although an authoritarian when the occasion called for it, Gladys had a heart of gold. Highly thought of and loved, not only by her customers, but throughout the entire village.

'Good morning Roy,' she said cheerily as she removed the beer mats from a table and sprayed it with polish before vigorously buffing it up with a duster.

'Morning Gladys. Have yer just got up?'

4

'I wish, yer cheeky buggger! I've been up since seven. Looking forward to yer day trip to Leeds today, or is that a daft question?'

'I certainly am looking forward to it, but if you're fishing fer a spare seat, sorry Gladys, it's men only I'm afraid.'

'Huh! As if. I see enough of you buggers every night o' the week. I'm looking forward to the peace and quiet.' She was about to ask where the other retrobates had got to - after all, they'd especially opened up early at their request - when Billy Gray, Roy's half cousin walked in. With his short cropped ginger hair, usually referred to as 'carrot heed,' at nineteen, he was a year younger than Roy. Accompanying him was Stuart Regent, who at twenty was the same age as Roy and also Roy's best mate.

'Good morning Mr an' Mrs C,' said a smiling Billy.

'Alright lads?' greeted John.

'Morning pet,' added Gladys. 'Ar thought fer a moment we'd opened up the pub exclusively on Roy's behalf.'

'Well thanks very much,' feigned a hurt Roy, his face like a scolded puppy. 'It's nice to feel wanted.'

'No offence hinny, but yer know what ar mean.'

'Divent worry Mrs Craig, Arthur, Dennis an' Don aren't that far behind us,' Billy assured her. 'They've just nipped in the shop for some fags an' newspapers.'

'What's up? 'Ave they run out of bootleg cigs an' baccy down the club?' asked John.

'Ar think they must 'ave,' said Stuart. 'That geezer that supplies 'em usually comes on a Sunday, but didn't show up this week.'

'They won't be happy paying full price then.'

'They'll probably be sharing a packet knowing them,' skitted Roy.

'Arthur Gray was Roy's grandad, who he lived with 'up the Square' along with his mother Kitty and grandmother Molly. Don Shand, a mate of Arthur's also lived up the Square which was only a few hundred yards from the Phoenix pub. Dennis Melly, Arthur's lifelong friend and fellow doorman at Stanhope Club, lived only a minute from the Phoenix on Front Street which in turn was only a stone's throw from the club. Aged sixty-two and three respectively, with Don the nipper of the trio at sixty. Don

5

and his wife Olga had moved to Stanhope in 1993. Originally from Sunderland, they'd moved for the cleaner air, Don having retired early from his painting and decorating job due to ill health.

'Well, yer canna blame folks getting their cigs an' baccy down the club if they're cheaper,' said John. 'It's ridiculous the amount of tax on a packet o' fags. It's no wonder there's so much smuggling going on from France. That cigarette machine of ours might as well be tekken out, the amount of use it gets. Yer pay full whack an' only get seventeen cigs. It's a bloody racket,' he carped as he emptied a crate of Newcastle Brown Ale, depositing the bottles on shelves behind the bar. 'I'd like to nar where all the brass gans. Bloody thieving, self-serving politicians. They're all in it to feather their nests at our expense. Ar wouldn't trust any of 'em as far as I could throw 'em - with the exception of Tony Benn, but he's retired now - more's the pity.'

'What have I told you about talking politics in front of me?' admonished Gladys.

'I'm sorry pet, but ar've got to get things off me chest,' said John defensively. 'Tek hospitals fer instance.'

'Oh, I give in,' sighed Gladys.

Unperturbed, John continued his tirade. 'You winna see any of them bent gets laid on a hospital trolley fer two days. An' if they're tekken ill, it won't tek 'em two years to see a consultant either, never mind how long it'll tek to actually get some treatment. The NHS is a bloody sham. No, ar'll tek that back - it's a scam. There's more managers than beds. An' these long waiting lists are created on purpose, so's people'll pay an' gan private. How can it be reet fer a sick person to wait years fer treatment? Many kicking the bucket in the process. But if you gan private, the same consultant can see you within days.' John was like a runaway express train now and nothing was going to stop him. 'Never mind all this massaging of figures, empty promises and lies constantly spouted by Blair's cronies. What New Labour were ganna do fer us when we re-elected them was nobody's business. Ar'll never vote again an' that's a fact. Hypocrites, the lot of 'em. In fact, they give hypocrisy a bad name. All on one big gravy train, the lot of 'em.'

'Come up for some air John man,' Roy advised him.

'I've started, so I'll finish young en. Just you hold yer horses a minute. What was the first thing New Labour - slash -Tories in disguise did when they were re-elected for a second term on a pack of lies?'

'I don't know,' yawned Gladys, 'But I'm sure you're gonna tell us.'

'Award their sens massive pay increases, that's what. God - ar mean Blair, the chosen one, granted himself a forty percent pay rise fer starters. Same with that legal department his parasitic wife works for - an' I use the term 'work' loosely. Syphoning off millions of pounds in legal aid. Tax payers money wasted. Representing paedophiles an' other low-lifes. Human rights . . . What aboot the human rights of the victims of these bastards? Who's representing them? No bugger, that's who! They're swept aside an' forgotten aboot while the scum are pampered over. All yer barristers an' solicitors an' the rest o' society's greedy dregs are laughing all the way to the bank!'

'John! When you've quite finished your party political broadcast on behalf of the Craig party, there's customers waiting to be served!' reprimanded Gladys sternly.

'Yes, o' course pet,' replied John sheepishly. 'What can I get you lads? The usual two pints o' lager is it?'

'Yes please John,' said Billy. 'An' our Roy's paying.'

'Like hell I am! I'm skint man,' lied Roy. 'Yer've more chance of a one legged cat burying a turd on a frozen pond.'

'Generous to a fault, that's your trouble,' muttered Billy.

Stuart was reading the lounge notice board. DAY TRIP TO LEEDS Saturday 10th May (men only) Included in trip:- Afternoon cultural tour of the city (pub crawl) Free bag of crisps (with little bag of salt) Crates of beer on sale at competitive prices. All welcome (with the exception of women and Roy Osborne) Coach leaves 11am sharp. Returns home 10pm. Tickets available at the bar £10

'Stewpot!' shouted Billy.

'Yeah?'

'There's a pint here bonny lad. Ar've bought 'em again.'

7

'Cheers mate, I'll remember yer in me will.'

'Never mind that, just mek sure yer get the next round in.'

'Aye aye sir,' saluted Stuart.

'You'll need plenty o' brass the fancy prices them city pubs charge mind,' said Gladys. 'Especially when you lot o' country bumpkins open yer mouths. Yer'll all be short changed fer wattered down beer.'

'No change there then,' muttered Roy. 'We might as well stay put.'

'What was that young Osborne?'

'Er . . . nothing Mrs Craig. I'm just off fer a Jimmy Riddle,' said Roy, edging off his bar stool before hastily retreating in direction of the gents. He wasn't going to be in the firing line if the landlady suddenly went off on one. He needn't have bothered because Gladys turned to her husband instead.

'And another thing John Craig, if you come rolling back here at all hours of the morning, off your heed on drink, divent come disturbing me, clattering about the bedroom an' wekking me up. In fact, come to think of it, you can sleep in the spare room an' then yer can wallow in yer own farts to yer hearts content. So think on mind.'

'Yes dearest. Message understood. Over and out.'

'An' less of the flippancy!' barked Gladys a little unconvincingly. Gladys only played at being an ogre. She was in fact, quite the opposite.

'What the hell's that racket?' exclaimed the landlord.

'It sounds suspiciously to me like your back door,' said Roy sarcastically. He had returned from the gents and was now nonchalantly flicking beer mats from the egde of the bar and catching them on the way down. "Ave yer got cloth ears man?'

'Whey, that's funny,' puzzled John leaving the bar. 'That back door should be oppen. You just stay sat there Roy, I'll get it. An' leave my bloody beer mats alone or yer barred!'

Roy wished he had a pound for every time John had hypothetically barred him.

The persistent hammering on the back door continued.

'Alright! Get thee pipe man, I'm on me way! No bloody patience some folks,' chuntered John as he unbolted the back door.

'Aboot bloody time too! Are you deaf or summat? My knuckles are red raw. What happened to oppening up at ten o'clock like? Too much o' the old ale last neet was it?'

'Less of yer lip Melly or yer'll be drinking ower the road in the Pack Horse. Mind, yer probably barred from there,' said the landlord as he let Dennis, Arthur and Don through the door. 'Besides, I've already oppened up once. Somebody's playing silly beggars an' I bet ar can guess who . . . Roy!'

'Bah! Someone's had a good clean out!' said Arthur, his hand covering his nose.

'Bah, yer not kidding,' agreed Dennis.

'Roy again,' decreed John, resignedly shaking his head.

'Smells like a rat climbed up his arse an' died,' added Don Shand, the third of 'Three Stooges' - so nick-named by Roy.

Gladys greeted them. 'Well, good morning gentlemen. We thought you'd got lost or been arrested.'

'Good morning to you too your highness,' returned Don. 'And how are you and that acid tongue of yours, this fine spring morning?'

'I'll be fine once ar get shut of ye set o' contrary old buggers. Roll on eleven o'clock, that's what I say. An' less of the "acid tongue" - slap-head,' said Gladys referring to Don's follicularly challenged head.

This brought guffaws of laughter from the young lads.

'We'd 'ave been here earlier Gladys,' said Dennis. 'But ar had to fill in Don's Lotto ticket on account of him being illiterate like. Yer nar what these macams are like.' (macam being a derogatory term for a person from Sunderland)

'Divent believe a word of it Gladys,' protested Don. 'It was Melly that held us up - gassing away to Cissie Brown behind Walter Wilson's counter. Talk the hind leg off a donkey once he starts prattling on.'

'Aye, tell me summat ar don't know,' agreed Gladys, who was now energetically polishing the large mirror above the defunct fireplace. 'He can talk fer England.'

'Ar resent that, landlady,' said an indignant Dennis.

'She's a queer bugger that Cissie Brown mind,' piped up Roy.

'An' how d'yer mek that out like?' questioned Dennis.

'Whey, ar went into the store last week an' asked her fer two pound o' bananas an' she said snootily, "Ar'll have you know they're called kilos now." Ar said, give us two pound o' kilos then!'

They all laughed.

'Very good Roy.'

'Thank you very much landlord. Ar reckon that joke deserves a free pint.'

'Nay, it wasn't that good,' said John. 'In fact, yer've more chance o' seeing Lord Lucan riding down Front Street on Shergar than of getting a free pint out of me.'

'Typical. Tight sod.' Roy turned to Dennis seeing as he wasn't getting any change out of John. 'Are yer after a bit on the side wi' that Cissie Brown then, yer dirty old man?'

'Yer joking!' exclaimed Dennis.

'Yer'd want a bag for her heed,' skitted Roy.

'That's uncalled for! Granted, she's no oil painting, but she's pleasant enough.'

'An' you'd be needing some Viagra to rise to the occasion, a man of your age.'

'I'd need a stick of bloody dynamite more like,' chuckled Dennis. 'Besides, I'd never be unfaithful to our lass - I love me house too much.'

'Ar've stopped doing that lottery,' announced John. What little brass they dole out goes to bogus asylum seekers an' lesbian an' puffter groups an' what 'ave yer. If it went to proper causes like our hospitals an' hospices or old folks homes, I'd still be buying the tickets, but stuff that fer a lark.'

'Ever the diplomat, John,' sighed Gladys. Don't sit on the fence will you?'

'Divent you worry pet, ar won't. There's enough sitting on it already. All this political correctness rubbish . . . Look where it's got us.'

'Aye, isn't that a fact,' tutted Arthur before ordering three pints of bitter. 'He's paying,' he said, nodding in the direction of Don.

'Nowt new there then,' grumbled Don, removing his wallet from his inside pocket. 'Get yourself one while yer at it John.'

'Well, thank you very much Donald. Ar'll 'ave half a Guinness with yer.'

'Funny that, how I get me Sunday name when I buy mine host a drink. How about you Gladys love, will you join me in a little aperitif?'

'He's talking aboot his knob again,' whispered Stuart to Billy.

'No thanks Don, I've chores to see to upstairs,' said Gladys, picking up her polish and duster. 'Ar'll leave you alcoholics to it then. Enjoy your trip.'

'Will do. Cheerio Gladys.'

'Give me a shout afore yer go John.'

'Will do hinny!' replied John, a touch of sarcasm in his voice. 'Phew, thank God for that!' he sighed, wiping the imaginary sweat from his brow with the back of his hand. 'I thought she was never ganna go.' Taking a spirit glass from the shelf, he poured himself a malt whiskey from one of the optics and knocked it back in one. 'Ah, that's better! Start as yer mean to go on, that's what I say. By the way, which of you pillocks was it bolted the back door?'

All eyes turned in the direction of Roy who was now perched on a stool in the corner of the snug bar.

'Who, me?' he smirked. 'As if I'd be so childish.'

'I'll swing for you one day lad,' John warned him.

'Gan on, divent be shy man.'

'No, I insist. After you old chap.'

'No, you first!'

Everyone looked in the direction of the hallway where the four 'old boys' had just come in. Tom Bellamy, Fred Brown, Ronnie Doyle and Unlucky Alf Smith - all of them now retired. Not that any form of hard work had ever played a major part in their lives. They'd always maintained that work was for fools and horses. And besides, it interfered with valuable drinking time. Their insistance in each allowing the other to enter the lounge bar first was not a gesture of gentlemanly conduct - far from it. The reason being was the age old tradition of whoever was first to the bar was obliged to put their hand in their pocket and stand the first round.

'Oh, get out o' the bloody road! We'll be here all day arguing the toss wi' you set o' skinflints,' snapped Ronnie, pushing his way past Unlucky Alf - who was so named because he had suffered a heart attack the night he won the Lotto - ironically, whilst drinking a can of Long-Life beer. At least according to Roy, so it must be true. Alf was in fact drinking a glass of his disgusting, prematurely fermented home-brewed bitter one Saturday evening whilst watching the Lotto on his ancient black and white television set. He always maintained he couldn't afford the extortionate colour TV licence. The first four numbers of his Lotto ticket had been drawn, thus resulting in a severe nervous stomach followed by an involuntary wet fart which soiled his moth-eaten long johns. Damaging enough in itself, but his biggest mistake was in taking a so-called mate - Tom Bellamy into his misguided confidence with regards to the unfortunate mishap. From that moment on it was only a matter of time before this supposedly clandestine information was relayed via the Stanhope grapevine to the ever tactful Roy Osborne. Alf might as well have broadcast it on the six o'clock news or advertised it on the front page of the Northern Echo because Roy's exaggeration of any gossip snippets he picked up were legendary. Nobody and nothing were out of bounds.

'Hey up, they're here!' announced John. 'The Last of the Summer Wine.'

'The Night of the Living Dead more like,' skitted Roy. 'I hope your hearse isn't blocking the car park - Joe's gotta get the mini-bus in.'

'Shut it Jaws,' said Fred, who needn't have wasted his breath.

'Alfred, 'ave yer picked yer 'osses fer today? Give us a quick gander, then ar nar which nags to avoid.'

'Yer can please yer sen what yer back son, but ar feel lucky today. Tek my advice though, if there's an 'orse called Big Gob-Shite, you stick yer brass on it.'

'Whoo . . . touchy! Hey, is it true Alf that the last time yer visited Leeds was with yer favver thirty years ago? You went to the City Varieties an' he passed away in his sleep when Max

12

Bygraves was on.'

'What a pathetic joke. Ar hope that's not yer best one.'

'Whey, there's plenty more where that came from.'

'Aye, ar thought there might be,' sighed Alf.

''Ave you lads been eating that Chinese muck again?' asked Tom. 'Cos it stinks to high heaven in 'ere.'

'Well yer can stick yer heed out o' the bus window then,' Roy advised him.

'Out o' the way everyone!' said Billy with some urgency, vacating his stool like Linford Christie off the starting block. 'Me Ruby Murray's deseperately seeking an exit!'

'Divent you be mekking a mess of my toilets mind!' called the landlord after him. 'Do yer nar, it's the same every weekend. Ar go through dozens of extra bog rolls. Ar'll 'ave to think aboot charging yer after yer first crap.'

'Whey, ar wouldn't put it past a miser like you,' skitted Roy. 'Are you sure yer not a Yorkshireman or a Jock? Anyway, it's easy for you to blame the tek away. Who's to say it's not your dodgy ale that gives us the trots? You're supposed to pull off the pipe cleaning fluid yer nar, not let it flow into our beer.'

'Arraway an' shite, yer cheeky sod. My pipes are spotless. Thoroughly cleaned every day, ar'll have you know. Yer divent get them 'Finest Ale' certificates on the wall behind your big fat heed fer nowt yer nar.'

'Get away, John man! Your lass prints them false certificates. Everybody in Stanhope nars that.'

'Do you want another drink in my establishment or what laddie?'

'Whey, that's very kind of yer landlord. Ar'll 'ave a pint o' lager an' whiskey chaser please,' grinned Roy. 'Oh, an' a bag o' salted peanuts.'

'Ar walked into that one didn't I? Oh, what the hell. Gan on, your next pint's on me seeing as it's a special occasion an' I'm in a good mood. There'll be nee chasers mind. If yer want a short, yer'll 'ave to buy yer own. I'll be lucky getting away wi' giving yer all a free pint without eagle-eyed madam upstairs noticing when she cashes up. Mind, she'll be 'aving the lasses round fer a shindig

13

tonight no doubt . . . Is your mother down tonight Stuart?'

'Aye.'

'Arthur?'

'Yes John, what can I do for yer?'

'Your Molly an' Kitty.'

'What aboot them?'

'Will they be down tonight?'

'Is Tony Blair a Tory? Course they'll be down. Yer can put money on it bonny lad.'

'Ar'll tek your word for it.'

'Ar wouldn't want to be here like when all the women get together. It'll be like a battery farm. All the hens clucking away at the same time. We're best out of it. They're worse than us blokes when they get ganning. An' by the time that lot's finished supping, your lass'll be up half the neet cashing up, so ar divent think a few pints'll gan amiss John.'

'Aye, yer probably reet Arthur, but yer not getting another free pint.'

'Yer canna blame a man fer trying.'

'How'd yer get on wi' that bird yer were chatting up last night Billy?' asked Roy. 'Did yer get yer tiny end away or what?' he smirked.

'None o' your business, nosey git. Anyway, a gentleman never tells on a lady,' said Billy, turning away with his nose in the air, fully aware of how frustrated Roy would be if he didn't get all the details.

'Ha way man, spill the beans an' divent spare the details.'

'My lips are sealed.'

'Arraway Billy man! Stop being such a stubborn pillock. I tell you aboot all my conquests divent ar? So, fair's fair. An' let's be reet Ginger, it's not that often you score with the chicks is it? Granted, she was partially sighted an' built like bouncy castle or yer'd never o' pulled her. But ar must confess, she didn't sweat much fer a fat lass.'

'Oh yeah . . . Well she did alreet driving me in her Porsche back to her luxury penthouse in Crook fer coffee.'

'Luxury pad in Crook . . . as if. Now ar nar yer tekking the piss.

14

Anyway, wherever it was she lived - did yer stay the neet? Everybody nars 'ganning fer coffee' means come an' slip me a length - granted, a small length in your case.'

'Get stuffed, yer jealous git.'

'Divent be like that bonny lad. Ha way, spill the beans, yer nar yer dying to,' coaxed Roy. 'Did yer drink from the furry cup? Yer nar . . . lick the beaver? Yer can at least tell me that much.' Roy leaned forward, 'It'll gan nee further than this room. Go on, whisper in me lug-hole. You've got my personal guarantee that ar'll be the soul of discretion.'

'Orh, give ower man! Try pulling the other one! Weardale's own town crier? You couldn't keep yer mouth shut if it were super-glued together!'

'I resent that accusation,' said Roy indignantly. 'Casting aspersions on my good character. They divent call me diplomatic Roy fer nowt yer nar.'

Roy gave up his fruitless quest of extracting information on Billy's carnal activities and returned to the morning paper, safe in the knowledge that after partaking of several alcoholic beverages, Billy's tongue would loosen to the extent that it would be in danger of falling from its moorings.

'Divent worry Royston,' whispered Stuart to Roy on his way to the gents, deciding a little mixing was in order, 'I nar all aboot Billy's bird an' she's a reet slapper. Ar have it on good authority, she's had more blokes than Ulrika Jonsson.' Leaving Roy more curious than ever, Stuart granted himself a wry smile.

'I divent nar, the euphemisms of todays youth are beyond me,' sighed Don. 'Get your end away, drink from the furry cup, licking the beaver . . . It all gans straight ower my heed, it really does.'

'Slides ower it more like - bald eagle,' skitted Roy.

'Just stick your snout back in that newspaper, clever dick. I'm talking to the organ grinders, not the monkey.'

'Please yer sen, Kojak, said Roy, continuing with the crossword. 'By the way Donald, who was it parted yer hair - Moses?'

'Nee respect or morals, the youth of today,' observed Fred. 'Kids of twelve an' thirteen up the duff . . . it's a bloody disgrace man. My mother would be turning in her grave.'

'Whey, yer canna blame 'em can yer?' pointed out old Tom. 'This stupid government handing out benefits on a plate. Rent free house an' council tax paid for 'em. Talk aboot easy street. It's not ganna encourage a work ethic is it? Young lasses dropping 'alf a dozen sprogs, all to different favvers. Think aboot it . . . all that family allowance every week. They must need a security guard to escort 'em from the post office. Sponging off the state all their lives while us senior citizens live on a pittance. It's no wonder them bogus asylum seekers are tripping ower their sens to get ower 'ere to soft touch Britain. They must think it's Christmas every day.'

Roy looked at Billy, rolled back his eyes, and let out an exaggerated yawn. 'Whey, ye old buggers 'ave room to talk, drawing yer big fat pension every week. The stoppages from my wages are scandalous. Ar've just had a long overdue pay rise, an' then that there Prudence Brown teks it all off me in National Insurance! Ar've ended up worse off than last year, an' what for? So you retired layabaouts can piss it up in the boozer all day. It's aboot time you society parasites snuffed it.' Roy sat back in readiness for the backlash. He didn't have to wait long because Tom obliged.

'Watch it, you sanctimonious little shite! You'll be old one day - if yer lucky. Yer've more lip than Leslie Ash.'

'Ar's immortal Thomas. Ar'll still be working in me eighties. Fit as a butcher's dog, me. An' ar'll still be pulling the birds. No Viagra for me . . . unlike ye geriatrics.'

'If you young uns did a bit more overtime an' paid more taxes, then us senior citizens might get a decent pension,' goaded Tom, thinking that two can play your game Roy. 'And for your information Sonny Jim, I can still stand to attention with the same upright vigour as when mount Vesuvius erupted.'

'You tell him,' encouraged Ronnie. 'How old are you now Tom anyway?'

'Seventy-four Ronnie, but ar divent look anywhere near it.'

'Four years older than me then.'

'Bloody hell, we've got Einstein in ower midst,' muttered Roy.

'Whey, ar tell yer what gentlemen,' said Ronnie. 'When we're down the club or at the town hall dance, it's always Tom that's surrounded by the ladies. He attracts 'em like flies round a cowpat. Mind you, ar do have it on good authority he's built like a stallion. Isn't yer nickname Dobbin, Tom?'

'Aye, 'tis true my good friend,' replied a grateful Tom, straightening himself up to his full height and sticking out his chest.

'What a load of bullshit!' scoffed Roy. 'Dobbin! . . . My little pony more like. He's built like a hamster. Ar've seen his shrivelled little pecker at the piss-stone. It looks about as much use as the pope's prick.'

'Just ignore him Tom lad,' advised Fred.

'Divent worry, ar will.'

'This beer tastes rank,' said Roy, pulling a face, handing his glass over the bar with just a small amount of lager remaining.

'Do I look stupid of summat?' said John. Don't answer that.'

'Just mek sure yer divent charge me fer me next pint an' ar'll let the matter drop. You wouldn't want the brewery finding out would you? So divent you be tekking advantage of my generous disposition.'

'That'll be two pund Osborne,' demanded John, placing a pint in front of Roy and holding out his hand.

Roy, begrudgingly handed over a five pound note. 'And divent be short changing me like yer do when I'm hammered. Do yer nar, I'm seriously contemplating tekking my valuable custom elsewhere.'

'Don't let me stop you. My life'd be a lot easier, I nar that.'

'That's as may be, but yer profits'd be right down.'

'True,' pondered the landlord. 'I think ar could live with that.'

'Just one more to finish me crossword,' said Roy. 'Any brainboxes amongst yer? Nar, daft question, just ignore me.'

'That winna be hard,' muttered Billy.

'Let's 'ave a butchers,' offered Unlucky Alf, putting on his glasses and bending over Roy to scrutinise the puzzle.

'It's nee good you trying to read that. Your eyesight's aboot as good as an American pilot's,' skitted Roy.

'Gan on Roy, read out the clue,' saidJohn.

'Oh alreet . . . To egg on - five letters.'

The room fell silent as they all pondered the conundrum.

'Got it!' announced Fred. 'Spur!'

'Give ower man,' derided Roy. 'That's only four letters an' anyway, I've got it - Toast!' he chortled.

'Whey, yer daft bugger,' said his grandad. 'Ar worry aboot you sometimes lad. Ha way John, fill 'em up. I'll buy a round in afore anyone else arrives.'

'Typical Arthur,' smiled John pulling a pint of bitter.

'Cheers Arthur,' echoed the group.

'You're welcome lads. It's the first an' last time ar get me hand in me pocket today mind.'

'You're quiet Stuart lad. What's up, got a hangover?'

'Nar, I'm just tired Dennis. Ar've been up since the crack o' dawn on me favver's milkround. I'll be reet enough though, ar'll get me heed down on the bus.'

'You'll be lucky wi' this rabble aboard.'

'By the way, speaking fer us young bucks,' proclaimed Roy. 'We would have much preferred a mixed outing wi' some young ladies along fer the ride. Listening to who's got the biggest leek on their allotment wears a bit thin after a few miles. A few lasses on board, primed with alcohol . . . ar could give 'em a large portion on the back seat. Or in Billy's case - a small portion. Mind you, the old boys'll probably get ower excited watching me in action. We'd 'ave to tek a paramedic along with us.'

'All mouth an' no trousers, that's ye young Osborne. You just watch a professional at work when we get to Leeds. Yer might pick up a few tips,' bragged Don.

'Oh aye, in yer dreams Yul Brynner. An' think on mind, divent you be hogging any karaoke machines on this trip. Yer wanna give other people a chance instead o' showing off. Folks were complaining again last night cos they didn't get a chance to sing.'

Though Roy would never admit it, Don was an accomplished singer when he had a microphone in his hand. With the voice of a tenor, between alto and baritone, Don was very popular with the ladies, which irritated his wife Olga somewhat because he was often besieged with requests on a Friday night at the Phoenix.

Happy to oblige most of the time, he would prefer now and again, to be left in peace and enjoy his pint with his mates. On one occasion when Don was halfway through a rendition of 'My Way' Roy had thrown a pair of his nana's bloomers at him. Hitting him full in the face, to everyone's amusement, Don had carried on singing as if nothing had happened. Reluctant at first, at Roy's request, Arthur had sneaked a pair of Molly's bloomers out of their bedroom. Molly wasn't aware of this until the following morning when she was down at the local shops where it was now common knowledge. Back home Roy was suitably chastised.

'What I'd like to know is who supplied our Roy with the bloomers in the first place!' She'd looked accusingly at her husband smoking his pipe, lounging in his favourite armchair by the fireside.

'Don't look at me! Not guilty your honour,' lied Arthur, burying his grinning face in his newspaper.

It was traditional at the end of Friday night's karaoke for the four old boys to get up and sing. This usually followed gallons of dutch courage as none of them were blessed with a singing voice like Don's. Known as The Four Flops by the locals, Roy preferred his own nickname of The Prat Pack and constantly took the mickey out of them. He'd advised Unlucky Alf against reaching the high notes in case he followed through. Silly advice really, thought Roy afterwards, there was more chance of Tony Blair dislodging his head from George Bush's arse than of any of them remotely striking a musical note. On one Friday evening, the Four Flops were murdering a rendition of 'Moon River' when Roy, somewhat worse for wear, dropped his kegs and mooned his bare backside at them, thus resulting in a severe reprimand from the landlord, but the regulars had thoroughly enjoyed Roy's antics. Not for the first time either, as the eccentric jester didn't believe in restraint. He had tried, with all the sincerity he could muster, to explain to John that he was only trying to add visual atmosphere to the song. "In that case," stated the landlord, "let's hope the old crooners divent attempt to sing 'Great Balls of Fire.'" If John had a pound for every time he'd given Roy a rollicking, he'd be a rich man. Though he'd never admit it, he realised just how much duller his pub would be without the roguish Roy. John was blessed more than most publicans were, in having plenty of older characters as customers, so having younger ones, especially Roy, was the icing on the cake. Most of the time anyway.

Chapter 2

'Ar's fairly confident of tekking first prize with my leeks an' veg this year, Arthur lad,' said Tom, referrring to the annual Stanhope Agricultural Show, which was staged every second weekend in September, come rain or shine.

'Oh aye, is that reet! How yer ganna achieve that like, after my twelve consecutive years of walking off with all the winning rosettes. What yer got up yer sleeve to mek any difference this year?'

'Whey, ar'll tell yer. Ar was surfing the net the other day an' ar came across secret tips fer growing prize vegetables.'

'How can it be a secret if yer came across it surfing the net? Whatever that means.'

'That is where, sadly, you lag behind Arthur. Being computer savvy, like my goodself, I nar where to search fer such things.'

'Unlike me yer mean, who canna be arsed wi' computers.'

'It's your loss Arthur.'

'Good luck then, bonny lad. But ar's quite content in sticking with my tried an' tested conventional methods. An' let's be reet, they've never failed me yet. Besides, you old bullshitter, if you knew what a computer looked like, yer wouldn't even nar how to plug it in.'

Tom laughed. 'Ar was just being hypothetical. Explaining what I'd do if ar had one.'

'That reminds me, talking of leeks, ar need to tek a piss,' said Roy, sliding off his stool.

'It's nice to see that finishing school yer sent your Roy to has paid off,' remarked Ronnie.

'Aye, he's a testimony to sophistication that lad,' said Arthur.

'Yer never nar, he might get his call up papers fer the next war. Must be one due . . . Syria . . . Iran . . . maybe North Korea?'

'If only Ronnie, if only. I'd even pay fer his equipment. He'll need some boots that divent melt fer starters, seeing as that ministry of deceit 'ave nee brass. 'Ave yer seen the news reports from Iraq? Bloody shameful what Bush an' Blair 'ave done to them poor people. Not content wi' blasting 'em to kingdom come with massive bombs, they're now starving 'em to death. Hospitals 'ave no medical supplies, or water even. Our great liberators 'ave left Iraq in a grip of lawlessness. They've let everything get looted, even the hospitals. An' all them ancient artifacts stolen an' smashed . . . Still, they've liberated the oil fields. Nee bugger'll get near them. An' what's happened to these weapons of mass destruction? Blair said Saddam was set to activate 'em at any minute. That excuse fer a man, our supposed saviour, must be the biggest liar to go down in history, an' there's been a few, ar can tell you.'

'So yer winna be voting fer him in the next general election I take it?'

'Too true Ronnie. Ar winna vote for any of them.'

'Why not change to Tory?'

'Cos they all shit in the same bucket man. Helping Blair push through his reforms . . . That bloke's more right wing than the British National Party. An' as for that Tory leader, I D S - Ian Duncan Smith! What sort of bloke 'as two Christian names? I ask you. He's got aboot as much charisma as the Duke of Edinburgh.'

'You sarcastic bitch Arthur.'

'Whey, yer've got to be. Ar was getting a bit carried away there. Canna let the bastards get yer down.'

'Here here,' agreed Ronnie.

'Divent despair Arthur,' said Billy, overhearing the conversation. 'According to your Roy, there's a chance you could be getting rid of him in the not so distant future.'

'Oh aye, an' how d'yer mek that one out Billy?'

'Whey, he was on aboot ganning to work in Iraq. Now it's had the shit bombed out of it, he reckons there'll be loads of building jobs.'

'He's nee chance,' stated Arthur scathingly. 'It'll be the Yanks that'll get all the work. Iraq'll 'ave plenty o' cowboys.'

'Ar heard that granda,' chelped Roy. 'Billy here might be a cowboy but yer canna tar me wi' the same brush. Ar've not been named Weardale's Master Builder of the Year fer nowt yer nar.'

'*Not*, being the operative word there,' muttered Billy.

'You've got a vivid imagination Roy lad,' skitted Dennis. 'If I needed any building work doing, I'd call Bob the Builder afore your shabby outfit.'

'Whey, that's just as well clever dick, cos it's no secret that you're as tight as a duck's arse and yer notorious fer paying yer bills late. The whole village nars it. Our firm 'ave got you blacklisted, so divent even bother contacting us if yer need any work doing.'

'There's nee danger of that young 'en. An' as fer yer ganning off to Iraq to bodge up the rebuilding . . . you an' Billy should be in the army there, waiting to invade Syria.'

'Ar canna afford it man.'

'What d'yer mean yer canna afford it?'

'Like me granda said, ower troops 'ave to buy their owm desert boots. American ones, ironically. The ones issued by the Ministry of Defence are cheap crap that melt in the heat. An' the guns divent fire neither, on account of 'em clogging up wi' sand! Fancy . . . putting sand in the desert . . . What next? An' if that's not enough, ower troops are more likely to be killed or maimed by 'friendly fire' from them trigger happy Yanks. Pilots, out o' their heads on speed bombing ower lads. It 'appened in the last Gulf War an' they assured us it wouldn't 'appen this time but, surprise, surprise - it did. Friendly fire . . . what a contradiction in terms that bugger is.'

Roy was on a roll, but now reverted to his usual, more familiar codswallop, his fertile imagination back in full flow. 'An' if that's not bad enough, to cap it all off, someone in their infinite wisdom has decided to burden ower troops with a visit from Davina McCall. Apparently she's ganning ower to entertain them - poor sods.'

'She'll be sore,' muttered Billy.

'What does she do then, sing?' asked Dennis.

'Nar, she just stands there with a microphone - though God knows why, cos she doesn't need one - an' then she shouts at you.'

'Is that all she does?'

'Hey, divent knock it Dennis man. It's made her a millionaire. Have yer not seen her every time yer switch yer telly on? She's always there, fronting the next phone-in programme.'

'Ah . . . come to think, ar know who yer mean now. Aye . . . yer reet Roy.'

'Too true I am.'

'How is it one person gets to front so many programmes? She's stopping other presenters getting a chance.'

'Easy . . . Give the TV chief a Monica.'

'A Monica?' puzzled Dennis. 'What's one o' them like?'

'A Monica Lewinsky,' stated Roy. 'Yer nar . . . as in Bill Clinton. Give the chief some head. Are yer with me now?'

'Oh aye,' pondered Dennis. 'Ar've got yer drift now.'

Dennis hadn't got a clue what Roy was on about but there was no way he was letting on.

'Do yer watch much TV Royston?' asked John.

'Only when they warn yer beforehand that the programme contains scenes of a sexual nature and extreme violence ,' he grinned. 'Ar saw a BBC statement the other neet. It said "In response to complaints that there are not enough of our ethnic friends on television, the BBC will now be showing Crimewatch twice a week." '

'Eeh . . . you're irredeemable Roy,' said John. 'Talk aboot un PC.'

'Stuff PC. I tell it as it is.'

'Are you sure yer not Bernard Manning's son?' said Don derisively.

'It's only a joke man! Whey, that 'Goodness Gracious Me' is always tekking the piss out o' the whites an' what about them all black music awards? Can you imagine if we 'ad an all white award - of any kind? They'd be screaming racial discrimination then. Ar divent give toss what colour any bugger is as long as they buy me a pint.'

'Your Eddie's coming with us isn't he Billy?' asked Stuart, referring to Billy's twenty-two year old brother.

'Nar, he can't mek it.'

'Aw, that's a shame, he's a good laugh is your Eddie.'

'Aye, yer nar what he's like ower kid, he never misses a good piss up usually, but he promised last week to tek me mam an' me auntie into Bishop, hospital visiting. He totally forgot aboot today's trip, an' when he realised he didn't like letting 'em down.'

Frank Nolan arrived. Recently retired from his heavy goods driving job, he was another life-long best friend of Arthur and Dennis and together with them was a member of the Stanhope Working Men's Committee.

'Hey up, it's Frank,' greeted Don. 'Yer managed to escape then?'

'Evidently,' came Frank's deadpan reply.

'How d'yer dodge your lass then? Did yer climb down the drainpipe or what?'

'Whey, buy us a pint an' ar might tell yer.'

'A pint of bitter for my good friend Frank please, mine host.'

'Ah, that's better,' gasped Frank after a long swig of beer, 'Ar was ready fer a drink. Me mouth's like the bottom of a budgie's cage,' he added, licking the froth from his lips. 'Cheers, my hairless friend. Why is it, beer always taste better when someone else is paying?'

'You're very welcome Franklin. Now ha way an' tell us how yer did yer Houdini.'

'What's a Houdini when it's at home?' asked Roy.

'You mean to tell me yer've never heard of the great Harry Houdini, the most famous escapologist of all time?'

'What's an escapologist?'

'What's an escapologist?' said Don incredulously. 'Ar don't believe it!'

'God, yer sound like Victor Meldrew.'

'Never mind aboot that, are yer seriously telling me yer divent nar what an escapologist is?'

'Don man,' piped up Ronnie. 'He's pulling yer chain.'

'Where was I before I was interupted?' said Don, looking daggers at Roy who was grinning like a Cheshire cat. 'Ah, yes . . . Frank. I thought you were grounded since that spot of after hours in the Grey Bull last weekend.'

'Whey, that's history now bonny lad. All watter under the bridge,' Frank assured him.

'That's not how ar heard it,' stated Don. 'My Olga bumped into your Jean in Walter Wilson's a couple o' days back an' by all accounts she wasn't a very happy bunny after your late night boozing session. An' she said she wasn't ower keen on letting yer loose fer today's trip either. What's changed her mind like?'

'Money, simple as that. Cost me a bloody fortune today has. She says "If you can fritter money away on booze, yer can give me some for me summer wardrobe," an' that's what she's doing now with ower Jane. They're over in Newcastle, knocking seven bells out o' my credit card. Shopping fer England, the pair of 'em an' here's me, an impoverished hen-pecked man.'

'Give ower, yer'll 'ave me crying in me beer. You must 'ave a tidy sum set aside, the money you've earned ower the years.'

'Is Frank giving you the poor tale again Don?'

'Aye, he is Dennis. But let's be reet, it's nowt new. Ar wish I were a hundred pund behind him. He keeps that Midland bank ganning on his own.'

'It's HSBC actually,' pointed out Frank, 'An' 'as been fer years. An' ar divent nar where you get yer information from, Dennis mixing Melly, I 'appen to be as poor as a church mouse. Ower lass 'as all the brass.'

'Pull t'other one,' scoffed Dennis.

'Ah, that's better,' said Roy, raising his behind from his stool and letting out a loud fart.

'Is there any need fer that!' berated John. 'Yer'd better not mark my stool. It's not long since we 'ad 'em re-upholstered!'

Roy's mobile phone which was on the bar with his cigarettes reverberated to the tune of Carly Simon's 'You're so Vain' - very apt for the conceited Roy. Stuart looked towards Billy, gesturing with his hand, implying that Roy was a merchant banker. Billy nodded his agreement.

'Hello! The Weardale Stud at your service!' answered Roy loudly before climbing off his bar stool and making his way to a quiet corner for some privacy.

'Bloody mobile phones. They're a damn nuisance,' carped Fred. 'A man canna have a pint in peace these days.'

'Ar'll second that. Ar say, ar'll second that,' said Tom.

'Not the Fred Elliot mimic again,' groaned Fred.

'He's right though,' said John totally in agreement. 'These mobiles are definitely the most unsociable contraptions ever invented. They can break up many an in depth conversation.'

'Then why divent yer ban the interminable things from yer premises John?' questioned Tom.

'Ar canna do that Tom man. I'd 'ave customers boycotting the place. And that, my friend, I can ill-afford. God knows, it's hard enough keeping our heads above watter as it is. Especially with Eastgate Cement Works shutting down.'

Blue Circle Cement works, a mile and a half up the dale in Eastgate had closed down it's works the previous summer. Being the mainstay for regional employment since the early 1960s, it was a massive blow for the villagers and local business establishments alike. Already, one of the four public houses in Stanhope was up for sale and had been for some months. If John had any intention of following similar action, he'd never mentioned it to anyone, but undoubtedly the closure of the cement works was playing at the back of his mind. "Wait an see," for the time being was his immediate motto. He'd cross any bridges when he came to them. Or as his wife would say, "Never trouble trouble, till trouble troubles you." Ever the philosopher was Gladys.

Alf looked up from his Daily Express, addressing anyone willing to lend an ear. 'Yer canna wonder Labour lost eight hundred plus seats in the local elections. To be honest, ar thought they'd lose a lot more. What, wi' council tax ganning up ten times the rate of inflation an' National Insurance tekken out o' folks pay packets . . Ar wouldn't mind so much if the money they robbed us of improved our public services, but they're worse than ever! Ar'll

27

never vote again, that's fer sure.' Alf looked about him in the hope of some endorsement.

Fred obliged. 'Yer'll not hear any arguments from me on that score.'

'Aye, yer reet,' agreed Ronnie. 'Blair an' his brown-nosers have destroyed this country in a matter of six years. Ar'll not vote again neither.'

'We don't live in a democracy anymore, it's a dictatorship lead by Blair the despot. Eeh, divent get me started,' said John, who hated Tony Blair and his cronies with a vengeance. 'You should try running a business under his regime. It's bureaucracy gone mad man. You wouldn't believe the paperwork that drops through my letterbox.'

'Talking aboot letters, you must be psychic cos you're just aboot to get another stack,' remarked Stuart who was peering out of the window. 'Postman Pat's on his way across the market place.'

'More bloody bills no doubt,' muttered John, leaving the bar to collect the post. 'Plus all the junk mail.'

'Postman Pat? Postman Jessie more like,' skitted Roy, now back on his bar stool. 'Bent as Boy George, yon bugger. He comes in here on a Friday night fer half a bitter an' a bag o' pig bollocks. Ar stay well clear of him. He's a knob voyeur - follows blokes to the bog to look at the size of their dick. I always gan in a cubicle when he's in. Ar've seen him eyeing John's arse when he's bent ower the tables collecting the glasses. Stuart talks to him a lot ar've noticed. Mind, ar've had me doubts aboot him fer a while an' all. Ar think he could be a fudge pusher.'

Stuart lashed out, 'Get stuffed yer lying get! Just because ar talk to him doesn't mek me a shirt lifter. He's alright is postie. Keeps him sen to him sen an' never bothers anybody - unlike some ar can mention.'

'Aye, he's always good as gold,' confirmed John. 'Comes into my establishment every Friday night regular as clockwork. Spends bugger all like. Four halves o' bitter, a bag o' scratchings, then back down to Front Street in Frosterley on the ten o'clock bus. He'd have a job on eyeing my backside anyway Royston, seeing as I employ a glass collector.'

'Of course, how silly of me. As if you'd be caught doing any real work. You're always stood gossiping at the bar. Socialising, as you like to put it.'

'Well, one has to keep the clientele happy with my rapport and witty, intellectual conversation bonny lad.'

'There's that smell again,' said Roy, sniffing the air. 'What can it be? Oh, I've got it - bullshit!'

'Well ar've heard that postie has a pund coin glued to his carpet,' stated Billy. 'So that when yer bend down to pick it up, he can ogle yer backside.'

'Hey up! Trigger's woken up with his usual time delayed comment. An' how come you nar postie's got a pund stuck to his carpet? 'Ave yer been to 'is gaff then?' taunted Roy.

'No, it were Stuart that telt us. Did yer slip him a length Stewpot?'

'Divent ye start Billy,' groaned Stuart. 'Ar've enough on wi' motor mouth there,' he said, nodding in the direction of Roy. 'Anyway, who was it you were talking to on the phone just now?'

'Whey, not that it's any of your business Stewpot, but if yer must nar, it was one of my female admirers, who else?'

'And what did she want?'

'Orh . . . just the usual . . . Another chick after me body. She reckons that if ar tek her out next week, she'll sit on me face back at her gaff afterwards.'

The old boys grouped together at the bar looked at one another in disbelief.

'And they say romance is dead,' said Fred.

'By, yer a smooth talking bugger Roy Osborne, ar'll give yer that,' said Tom.

'Whey, thanks fer the compliment,' said the smug, self-satisfied wind-up merchant. 'One tries one's best. If they could bottle my charisma, ar'd be a millionaire. That reminds me - ar'd better nip to the bog an' pick up a couple o' packets of them extra large Durex. They divent nar it yet, but those lucky Yorkshire mingers are in fer a real treat.'

'I bet they can't wait,' skitted Billy.

'Ar'll 'ave another tom-tit while I'm there an' all.'

'Do yer mind?' reproached Tom. 'Too much detail son, too much detail.'

'Hey, Roy! Afore yer gan in, tell 'em what yer best chat up line is,' encouraged Billy. 'They can try it out in them lap dance clubs in Leeds then.'

Roy sighed, 'Gan on then, if ar must. Ar'll give yer one of me quick ones, but believe me, it'll tek more than a few words from a pervy geriatric to impress the ladies. Reet, listen up . . . My goodself, the master puller, will casually walk up to a bird - in this case, a Yorkshire slapper - although I must stress at this point, they usually walk up to me.'

'Yeah, alright God's gift to women, just get on with it,' snapped Billy.

'Patience, my little ginger pal. All good things come to those who wait,' said Roy with slow deliberation. 'An' divent you be getting a stiffy during my yarn. Now, where was I? Ah yes, back to the plot me thinks. As ar was saying - I'll walk up to a bird . . . '

'Talking of birds,' interrupted Alf, 'you've just reminded me. Do yer remember when pubs had parrots an' mynah birds in the bar an' all the locals would teach 'em to swear?'

'Alf, stop meandering! Yer as bad as Roy,' censured John. 'Roy, carry on afore I lose the will to live.'

'Right. Well, ar'll walk up to a chick an' say, "Excuse me pet, 'ave yer got a mirror in yer knickers because ar can see meself in 'em later." '

'An' then he gets a slap round the heed,' skitted Stuart.

'No ar divent clever twat! It works a treat every time. They think "What an original chat-up line, I must take this gorgeous Brad Pitt look-a-like home with me so's he can shag me silly." '

'Eeh, yer'd think he invented sex the way he gans on,' mocked Ronnie. 'What's it like in that little world you live in?'

'Same as yours but a lot more exciting thanks. Live fer today, that's my motto. Ar've nee intentions of living to a ripe old age stuck in some cockroach infested private nursing home, sucking on a piece of milky bread, pissing me sen an' sleeping in a soiled bed. One bogus asylum seeker looking after thirty old farts, slipping us gorilla tranquillisers to stop us from being a nuisance

30

wandering aboot an' shitting in wardrobes. Stuff that fer a lark.'

'Yer may not 'ave a choice in the matter son. It depends on what life deals you,' said old Tom. 'Some old folks 'ave caring relatives to look after them. Others, like meself are less fortunate. An' speaking for meself, ar only hope ar divent get a debilitating illness. Aye,' he pondered, 'A massive fatal heart attack'll dee me. Preferably supping a pint of ale here in the pub or club. Then, ar's not a burden to anyone. But like ar said, it's the luck of the draw kid.'

'Hold up fellows, we're getting a bit morbid here aren't we?' remarked John. 'This is a rare day off fer me, so let's lighten up eh?'

'Aye, yer reet John,' said Fred. 'Ar tell yer what, get yer sen a whisky an' what everyone else wants.'

A roar of approval chorused around the lounge, while Roy, feeling Fred's brow for any signs of fever said, 'Are you feeling alright old boy?'

'Carry on an' yer'll buy yer own ale bonny lad.'

'Just joking,' genuflected Roy. There were no depths he wouldn't sink to in pursuit of a free pint. 'It's that old Tom that's always moaning on aboot having every illness going. Only last week he went fer another medical. "Go on doctor, tell me the worst," he whined. "You're a hypochondriac," said doctor Patel. Tom said, "Oh no, not that as well!" ' Roy chortled, mildly amusing the tribe.

Tom chose to ignore Roy's jibe and turned to John. 'Here yer are landlord,' he said, handing him a piece of paper. 'Ar've picked four 'osses. All winners wi' a bit o' luck,' he added with a wink.

'Hold on to it until we get on the bus man,' whispered John, looking round furtively. 'Our lass could walk in any minute.'

'Aye, alreet. Ar'll give it yer later then.' Tom pocketed the home-made betting slip.

Unbeknown to his wife, John had been taking horse racing bets for the last twelve months or so, personally paying out any lucky punters and pocketing the losers bets. So far, it had proved a profitable enterprise. The only bookmakers in Stanhope had closed down in the mid nineties. Although this practice was

31

illegal, John was not the only licensee taking a risk in this venture. Obviously, he kept these clandestine dealings from Gladys, because if she ever found out there'd be blue murder. Not least because they would almost certainly forfeit their liquor licence. With competition being so cut-throat, John decided the risk was worth taking financially speaking, but it was a close call. However, having built up a tidy nest egg for his and Gladys's retirement, if he stopped work tomorrow, he'd not lose any sleep. In fact, long lazy days fishing on the riverbank, coupled with frequent trips to his favourite locations scattered around the beautiful Scottish Highlands, John's very own Garden of Eden - would suit him down to the ground. His special favourite spot being the breathtaking Loch Maree in the Western Highlands. The loch, in an idyllic isolated location some ten miles away from the nearest village of Kinlochewe was dotted with dozens of tiny islands and was surrounded by impressive mountains. The icing on the cake was the Loch Maree Hotel, built in the early eighteen hundreds and sighted right at the water's edge.

John had many memories of the area, all of them happy ones and his enthusiasm of the Highlands was shared by his wife Gladys who sometimes accompanied him on the trips. They'd both fallen in love with the quaint hotel right from the start and would go off on daily jaunts to Ullapool and Plockton, the Isle of Skye and the stunning Torridon mountains. Another favourite was Poolewe with its beautiful Inverewe Gardens.

They were spoilt for choice amidst such natural beauty and though John genuinely enjoyed these breaks with his beloved wife, he would be the first to admit that fishing the vast Loch Maree with his mates was the ultimate canine's bollocks. Whenever it was possible - usually at the drop of a hat - Frank, Arthur, Dennis and Don would clamber aboard John's pride and joy, his Chrysler Voyager people carrier. The fact that two of the men didn't even own a fishing rod mattered not. So long as three or four crates of Newcastle Brown Ale accompanied the party, all was well. The only fly in the ointment on these trips had to be the infamous Scottish midges, hovering round you - some folks more than others - like flies round a compost heap. Swatting the bothersome insects was futile. Midge repellent was the only answer. A good dollop applied to any exposed areas did seem to deter the pesky mites.

After the Stanhope party has settled themselves in the Loch Maree hotel, they would then employ for a fee, the services of a ghillie (a fisherman with knowledge of the best fishing ground to cover) who had been ingeniously nicknamed Jock by the quick witted Weardalers. He was a jovial affable man, always up for a laugh and joke and, given the opportunity, would hit the bottle with them into the wee small hours of the morning.

The results of their fishing produced wild salmon which were kept in a keep-net at the side of the sixteen foot boat. The abundance of fish throughout the loch always made the expeditions a resounding success. Even the less able fishermen always managed to hook a fish or two before getting down to the more serious business of sampling some of Scotlands finest malts. Naturally, these would be followed by Newcastle Brown chasers and complemented with the customary picnic basket of Angus beef sandwiches and copious packets of crisps. If heaven existed, surely they'd found it here.

On one occasion two years ago, there was a mini crisis when Fred, a little worse for wear having knocked back one dram too many, had unfortunately fallen over board while relieving himself in the loch. Luckily, he was an accomplished swimmer. Immersed in the depths of the freezing water, he was soon shocked from his drunken stupor. A few breast strokes, he was scrambling aboard the boat, declining a helping hand from his mates - which was just as well since they were doubled up with laughter and about as much use as a chocolate fireguard.

Back on shore, the netted salmon they caught would be transferred and kept alive in two giant tanks at the back of the hotel. Then on the morning of their departure, the fish would be put into cool boxes provided by John, thus ensuring a component of freshness on the return journey home. Back in Stanhope, they would each take an equal share. John had his regular home market - selling them on to other publicans. There was never a shortage of customers for any fish surplus to requirements either.

These would be snapped up within the hour at Stanhope Club.

'Where we meeting up with your Alistair?' asked Frank.

'Whitelocks pub,' replied Roy. 'Yer nar - on Briggate in Leeds. We've been there afore.'

'Wye aye man. Ar nar where yer mean. If ar recall, they keep a canny pint mind.'

'Ar'll not argue wi' that Frank.'

Alistair was Arthur's eighteen year old grandson and cousin to Roy. Living in Leeds, he'd arranged to meet up with them in the Whitelocks pub in Turks Head Yard, which was named after a former inn licensed in 1715 but occupied by Whitelocks First City Luncheon Bar since 1880. Having one of the best Victorian pub interiors in the city, elaborately decorated with faience tiles, carved mirrors and polished brass fittings. It's dining area, which retains all the best traditions of English pub catering, is reknowned for it's roast beef and Yorkshire Pudding.

Alistair had booked two weeks holiday from his job as a trainee burglar alarm engineer and was returning with the day trippers to Stanhope that evening. He could hardly contain his excitement and was looking forward to staying at his nana's and grandad's. Unfortunately, there was Roy to contend with, but you can't have everything.

'All you old 'ens . . . ' piped up Roy, summoning the old boys attention.

'Senior gentlemen if yer don't mind son,' corrected Unlucky Alf.

'Okay, as you wish,' chuntered Roy. 'All you senior gentlemen - as if - should 'ave wives waiting at home for yer.'

'Oh aye, an' pray tell us, o wise one of the north east, how the hell that would be to our advantage. We'd lose ower freedom fer a kick off,' pointed out Fred.

'Because . . . if you contracted that Alzheimer's disease, then you'd wake up to a new woman every morning.' Roy waited for the penny to drop while Stuart and Billy, having heard the joke many times before looked at each other reservedly. Being more considerate than their overbearing brash mate, they didn't want to offend any of the old boys.

'Orh . . . I get it,' said Fred with slow deliberation. 'Cos yer memory goes . . . an' yer wouldn't know it were yer wife. Very good young Osborne. A bit morbid, but clever.'

'Ar think a lot of hen-pecked husbands'd like to swop the old battle-axe every morning,' remarked Tom.

If Roy had been expecting some outcry at his distasteful comments, then the old boys were reluctant in giving him any gratification.

Billy, unwittingly threw Roy a lifeline. 'Do yer George Bush impersonation Roy.'

'It doesn't contain cheap jibes at the female genitalia does it?' asked Frank.

'No clever clogs, it doesn't.' Roy cleared his throat with an exaggerated cough. 'Reet, here goes, "No siree, this is only the beginning. After we've bombed the shit out of Eye-raq, we'll move on and bomb Tie Rack. And hell, if needs be we'll go on and bomb Celine Dion. *That's not a country sir, it's a singer.* No matter, we'll goddam bomb him anyway. Let's not take any chances here boy. This is war. You're with us or against us." '

The group laughed. Roy could be funny on the odd occasion.

'Time's moving on gentlemen, it's gone a quarter to eleven,' announced the landlord. 'I suggest yer all pay a final visit to the gents afore we hit the road.'

'Whey, there's loads o' time yet,' grumbled Fred.

'Will yer lend the old boys a pair o' scissors while they're in there John?'

'What are yer chelping on aboot now Roy?'

'Whey, they could all do wi' cutting off some o' that nasal an' lug 'ole hair they've got dangling. Put it together, yer could fill a ruddy mattress with it. We canna have 'em embarrassing us on this cultural visit to Leeds. Like it or not, we're all ambassadors for Stanhope and the north east.'

'You? Embarrassed?' skitted John. 'That'd be a first.'

'True, that was just a load o' bollocks. Life's too short to hold back John man. That's my philosophy. Eeh . . . do yer remember last years trip to Manchester? What a day that was. I ended up pissed as a newt.'

35

'So, what's new?' said Billy.

Roy ignored the comment and went on. 'Do yer remember? We went on the usual pub crawl an' got split up fer some reason, an' then Alf went missing. I'd gone into Argos to buy a new watch an' Alf was in there, pencil an' order slip in one hand, looking through the catalogue thinking he was in the bookies! He looked up at the screen there an' ended up putting a tenner on 'out of stock!'

'You divent 'alf come out wi' some twaddle lad,' said Roy's grandad.

'Could yer not 'ave left him at home Arthur?' asked Frank.

'If only. Our Molly an' Kitty would insist he came along. Said they needed a full days recuperation. In fact, his mother told me to leave him in Leeds.'

'I'm not listening to this crap!' came Roy's response, leaving his stool to make a final visit to the increasingly busy gents toilet.

John opened a packet of Hamlet Cigars and lit one up. Drawing on it, he exhaled with a contented sigh. After years of smoking sixty Capstan Full Strength every day, he'd finally decided to quit, with great difficulty, some five years ago. After losing several good friends and customers through lung cancer, he now restricted himself to the odd Hamlet on special occasions, such as today.

'I tried packing in the ciggies an' smoking cigars like you John,' stated old Tom. 'Lasted two days. Ar were that bloody miserable ar went an' bought twenty Woodies. Ar must 'ave chain smoked the first ten. It were sheer heaven,' he reflected, picking up his two handled silver tankard. Tom was in the early stages of Parkinson's disease and with the involuntary shaking of his hands, the two handled tankard purchased by John on a recent visit to Newcastle had proved a godsend. Being one of his first ever customers and now a dear valid friend, the landlord had a soft spot for old Tom. Single, as were the other three old boys, Tom had a younger sister, Mary, who lived just a few doors from him. She popped in every day to check on Tom, taking his washing or doing any shopping and cleaning that was necessary. Tom adored her and was always buying her chocolates or flowers to show his appreciation.

Gladys entered and, to the cheers of the customers, put a large plate of beef sandwiches on the bar. 'Don't say I never give you anything,' she said smiling.

Roy was returning from the gents fiddling with his crotch area. 'Boston Strangler's not dead,' he chuntered. 'He meks flippin' underpants. Hey up! Sarnies!' he said, spotting the plate on the bar. 'What are they, salad?'

'Beef,' stated John.

'Gladys, 'aven't yer done any salad sarnies?'

'No, they're all beef.'

'Whey, that's nee good to me, I'm vegetarian,' stated Roy. 'Ar divent want to end up wi' mad cow disease.'

'It's a bit late fer that,' muttered Gladys.

'Orh, gan on, ar'll 'ave beef then. Beggars can't be choosers,' said Roy tucking in. 'Divent worry aboot Shakin' Stevens here, ar'll feed him,' he said referring to old Tom. 'Yer divent want crumbs an' bits of old beef on yer freshly hoovered carpet.'

'You leave my Tom alone bugger lugs,' said Gladys, putting her arm around old Tom and giving him a kiss on the cheek.

'Tek no notice of 'im Gladys, he's just jealous,' grinned Tom, who was in his element.

'Ar'd watch your lass wi' Casanova there John,' said Roy. 'His legs are knocking together like a pair o' castanets. Watch yer divent crush Dobbin, Tom!'

'Trust you to lower the tone, midden mouth,' berated Gladys. 'How this lot puts up with you all day is beyond me. I'd end up throttling yer.'

'Put up with me?' said Roy incredulously. 'Your John never leaves my side. He's always hanging aboot me, trying to pick up one o' my cast offs. He's like a dog wi' two tails on these trips Gladys. One o' these days he'll not return, but sail off into the distant sunset with a dusky maiden on his arm, never to be seen again.'

'Well can I 'ave that in writing,' said Gladys nonchalantly. 'Anyhow, with that hopeful thought, I'm off. A woman's work is never done. See you all later.'

'Cheerio my beloved,' crawled John before retrieving his glass of whisky from under the bar and taking a drink. 'Thank God for that.'

Roy sat next to Stuart and Billy.

'It's a bit late joining us now, we're off in a minute,' said Stuart.

'Ar was busy winding 'em up at the bar. That, an' sorting out my heed wi' the hair o' the dog. It was fair thumping early on. It's amazing what a few pints does. Ar feel great now. Bring on the day, I'm raring to go. Wicked man,' said Roy, clicking his fingers, Ali G style.

'Ar must admit I was a bit worse fer wear an' all this morning,' said Billy. 'A pint o' watter an' an 'alf hours walk wi' the dogs, ar felt a lot better. Like ye Roy, a few bevvies an' I'm primed.'

'There's no point asking if you were suffering this morning is there?' said Roy referring to Stuart.

'Correct. I've got the constitution of an ox,' boasted Stuart.

It was well known that Stuart didn't suffer hangovers, which was just as well being a milkman and up with the lark six days a week. He worked with his father who had built up the expansive business over thirty years. At the tender age of ten, Stuart had been out delivering milk on a Saturday morning and mid week in the school holidays. He wasn't afraid of the hard work or the early mornings, but the expectations of him taking over the family business in the not too distant future didn't lie well on his young shoulders. He wanted more out of life. Computer literate, he saw a whole new world of opportunity out there. He'd already noticed the slight decline in the business but had never expressed any concern to his father. It was only the odd cancellation here and there, but significant none-the-less. Maybe his father had become a little blinkered after thirty years and unwittingly took his milkround too much for granted, while Stuart was more aware of any future impending uncertainties regards the business. He also felt that the recent closure of Eastgate Cement Works could prove to be the final nail in the coffin. Most of the older, long term customers felt a sense of loyalty in buying from their regular as clockwork, trusty milkman, but Stuart could foresee the change in attitude of the younger customers who would have no qualms in cancelling their daily pinta and go buy in bulk, much more cheaply from the supermarket. Maybe it would be a blessing in disguise, he reflected, especially as his enthusiasm for the job lessened daily.

"Ave yer seen old Tom's face?' said Roy. 'He's beaming like Blackpool Illuminations. He loves all that attention Gladys gives 'im yer nar. His face is a picture when she's fussing round 'im. He's a wily old bugger mind - but that Alf's got 'im weighed up to a tee. When it's Tom's turn at the bar, his shakes escalate like hell an' he kids he canna get his wallet out. But Alf's 'aving none of it - he's in there like a rat up a drainpipe. He whisks Tom's wallet out of 'is inside pocket quicker than the Artful Dodger.'

'Eeh, you're incorrigible Roy,' chuckled Stuart. 'Nowts off limits as far as you're concerned, is it?'

'Correct, my good friend. But the old boys nar what ar's like, an' they can give as good as they get.'

'Yer a fraud an' all Roy,' said Billy accusingly. 'Cos it's all a front yer put on. Ar've seen yer sending over the odd pint to old Tom - an' the rest o' the old boys come to that.'

'Ar divent do I?' said Roy, feigning innocence. 'It must be when ar's pissed. Divent tell anybody mind, ar've a reputation to maintain. Besides, if I'm a bit short on a Thursday neet, ar get the odd pint sent ower from the old lads. Apart from Fred that is - he's as tight as a bull's arse in fly season, yon bugger.'

'Talking of bull's behinds - are yer still ganna support that excuse fer a football team now they're down in the first division?' skitted Billy referring to Roy's favourite team, Sunderland who had just been relegated due to finishing at the bottom of the Premiership League after a dismal season. Both Billy and Stuart had been walking about with a self-satisfied smugness for months now, as their team, Newcastle United had excelled themselves in the season. Finishing third in the Premiership, they'd qualified for the next seasons Champions League and would be competing with other top teams in Europe. To say the lads had given Roy some stick would be an understatement unparalleled, having taunted him without mercy. It had to be said, this was much to the delight of everyone - Roy getting a dose of his own medicine. In his typical bullish manner, he had emphasised it was only a game and that it was irrelevant anyway, seeing as he'd changed his allegiance and was now supporting Manchester United, who just happened to be the Premiership champions. Obviously, this absurd announcement had been dismissed with the disdain it deserved. Roy had purposely selected Manchester United as his new team in the knowledge that they were hated with a passion by all the fanatical north east football fans - and virtually the rest of the country if the truth be known. A victim of their own success you might say. Billy had criticised Roy, maintaining that a true football supporter would stick by his team through thick and thin. Billy, along with Stuart, was a testament to this statement having faithfully supported Newcastle United for the last twelve years. Not just through their present good times, but also the none too recent leaner times. Roy had hoped to find some consolation by way of Alistair's home team Leeds United joining Sunderland in Division One, but a Leeds 3-2 win the previous Sunday had put down any aspirations in that direction. The result had ensured their Premiership survival with a game to spare. There again, Alistair wouldn't be shouting from the rooftops. His team might have narrowly escaped relegation, but considering the quality of their highly paid players, Leeds United had performed abysmally. Finishing a disappointing fifteenth in the final league placings, and the unlikelihood that any of the top players would be left in the club after being sold on in the closed season, things were looking ominous for the foreseeable future. Alistair would not be renewing his season ticket.

Chapter 3

Arthur glanced at his watch, 'Two minutes to eleven. Better not order another pint - Joseph's always punctual. Ar'll wait till we're on the bus an' break out a bottle then.'

'Give us another packet o' them expensive nuts an' raisins will yer John?' said Don.

'What d'yer mean expensive?' protested John, taking down a packet from the card on the wall. 'A man's gotta mek a living yer nar.'

'Yeah, but wi' your prices, yer tekking the piss man. They're half the price at Safeways in Consett.'

'Whey, go gan an' get 'em from there then! Ye buggers divent have a clue - the massive overheads ar have.'

'Give ower! Yer'll 'ave the violin out next. You must be the richest landlord in Weardale.'

'Ar wish.'

'That's your third bag o' nuts an' raisins,' commented Frank. 'Divent yer get fed at home or summat? When you 'ave a dump, yer turds must come out like Picnic Bars.'

Everyone laughed.

'Not that I have to justify my eating habits to ye,' said Don indignantly, 'But if yer must nar, ar had a full English this morning. These pub snacks help to soak up the ale, especially when yer in fer a long session like today. That's what ar read somewhere anyway, an' ar find it works fer me.'

'Aye, yer reet Don,' said Arthur in agreement. 'After I've tekken dog fer a good walk up the dean, I tuck into a good breakfast when ar get back. Then aboot nine o'clock, ar sup a pint o' milk to line me stomach - afore a major piss up that is. Like you bald eagle, it does the trick fer me.'

'Ar canna stand milk,' shuddered John, 'It meks me gip. I only sup black coffee. Ar divent even bother wi' tea. In fact, ar can sup all day wi'out eating owt. I'm lucky in that respect. I'll be dining out today mind,' he said, smacking his lips. 'Yorkshire Pudding wi' roast beef an' onion gravy. Yer canna beat Whitelocks nosh. Highlight of the day by a long mile.'

'Give ower man, me mouth's wattering already.'

'As long as yer divent dribble all ower my bar, I'm not bothered. Hey up! The chauffeur's arrived! 'Are yer alreet big fellow?'

'Aye, fair to middlin' John,' replied Joseph, the mini-bus driver. 'Are we all ready fer the off then?'

'Just aboot. There's a few stragglers in the gents like. Where yer parked - round the back?'

'Got it in one,' came Joseph's laid back reply.

At six foot two and fifteen stone plus, Joseph was not a man you'd want to mess with, but he was normally a gentle giant and slow to temper. Some months earlier, a local chancer, a little worse for wear having been on a cocktail of booze and other chemicals, had pushed his luck a little too far. After insulting Joseph more than once, the foolish lad was unceremoniously deposited spark out on the Phoenix lounge carpet. Removed from it by his more *compos mentis* companions, he was carried home for a spot of convalescence. Not surprisingly, Joseph had not encountered any hostility since from the lad in question - or anyone else for that matter.

'Do yer want a drink Joe?'

'Aye, I will please - I'm a bit parched. Ar'll 'ave a Brtitvic 55. Cheers John.'

Joseph Haynes drove buses locally for a living, but when the Phoenix were having a day trip he always booked a days holiday well in advance. It was literally a busman's holiday, but this suited Joseph as he enjoyed these varied excursions. Apart from the tax-free benefits his bit of moonlighting accrued, he got to visit the different cities and coastal resorts. On reaching whichever destination, he would park up for the day and tag along with the rowdy party for a while before slipping away to take a look at the local landmarks, museums and art galleries etc. He liked a little culture did Joseph, and all with the added bonus of being beyond his wife's nagging for the day. Not that his wife was bothered anyway, because she too would be making the most of the day. She'd be down at the Phoenix come evening, living it up with the lasses. A good little drinker, Jean could keep pace with the best of them. At forty-five, the same age as her husband, the wiry little brunette had the liver of an ox. The woman could drink for England and every Saturday night, she did. Gladys didn't mind, quite the opposite, because the more Jean drank, the more comical she became. She was the life and soul of any social gathering. There was just the one occasion when Jean had drunk that little bit too much and had to be carried upstairs to sleep it off in the spare bedroom. This was no bad thing being that she was the pub cleaner. Singing as she worked, she was bight as a button next morning. Hangovers seemed to by-pass her.

'Stuart! Billy!' shouted John.

'Yes boss!'

'Pop these crates o' broon ale on the bus will yer? Roy'll bring the sick bucket!'

Knocking back the contents of their glasses, the lads went over to the bar at Johns bidding. The landlord supplied the bottled beer free of charge on these outings. 'Loyalty ale' as he put it. 'Stale ale' was Roy's sentiment, depending on how scrutinising Gladys had been of late regards turning of the stock. John usually managed to sneak out a couple of bottles of the famous grouse whisky as well.

Knocking back the last dregs of his lager, Roy went behind the bar and picked up a bucket with two bottle openers in the bottom.

'Here, stick these two bottles o' whisky in,' said John putting them in the bucket and covering them with a bar towel. 'Get 'em out to the bus sharpish afore her ladyship finds out.'

'Okay, get thee pipe man. What did yer last slave die of?' chuntered Roy. This was the third year in succession he'd carried out the sick bucket. For some reason, Roy was the unofficial bucket carrier. It was probably due to the fact that the bucket was a lot lighter than the crates of Brown Ale. Hard work never killed anybody, but why take the risk? That was Roy's philosophy anyway and he was sticking to it.

On his way out to the minibus, Roy bumped into Alf coming out of the gents. 'Alf man!' he exclaimed, looking at his head. 'Yer Irish jig's lopsided. Nip back in the bog an' check it out in the mirror.'

Alf had worn a toupee for the past two years. After enduring the initial varied comments by all and sundry at the Phoenix - Roy the main protagonist as usual - Alf had eventually established a degree of comfort with his new look.

'Yer'd better not be winding me up laddie.'

'I'm not! Honest Alfred. If yer've run out of superglue, yer welcome to use some of my masticated chewing gum,' offered Roy, stretching the gum from between his clenched teeth.'

'Stick it back in yer gob, yer mucky git!'

'Divent be such a prude Alfred man. Beggars can't be choosers . . . Alfred man . . . ' pondered Roy. 'Wasn't there a group called that?'

'Manfred Mann, yer divvy - but what's that got to do wi' owt? Anyway, shove off wi' yer bucket, I'm off to finish me ale.'

'On your head be it,' grinned Roy.

'Yer canna resist can yer? Get ganning or yer'll feel the back o' my hand,' warned Alf, raising his arm to a fleeing Roy who was laughing like a demented hyena.

'That grandson o' yours Arthur . . . Can yer not tape 'is mouth shut or summat? Is me 'airpiece on reet?'

'It looks alright to me,' said Ronnie.

'It's not lopsided or owt?'

'No, it's fine,' Ronnie assured him. 'Apart from it being a bit grimy that is. Hey, John!'

'Yes Ronnie.'

' 'Ave yer got a saucer o' milk for Alf's syrup? To perk it up a bit like!'

Noisy laughter ensued at Alf's expense.

'Yer rotten lanky bastard! An' ar thought you were a friend o' mine.'

'Alreet, keep yer 'air on!' chuckled Ronnie.

'That reminds me,' said John. 'Ar've a dead rat to shift out o' the cellar afore ar go.'

Alf groaned. 'That's it, I'm off on the bus. Ar'll see you set o' bairns later. It's like a bloody kindergarten in 'ere!' He stormed out of the lounge with a face like thunder.

'Do yer think we've gone a bit OTT?' questioned John.

'Nar,' said Ronnie. 'He'll be reet. Just 'aving one of 'is juvenile strops. It winna last long. A wee dram on the bus an' he'll be fine. Mebbe we'd better refrain from the toupee jokes the rest o' the day. Everyone agreed?'

'Aye,' they concurred.

John opened the door to the upstairs living quarters. 'I'm off now pet!' he shouted. 'Ar'll drop the back door latch on me way out!'

'Okay!' replied Gladys. 'Enjoy yer sen, but think on, divent gan ower the top!'

'There's no danger of that my beloved! Bye!'

'Cheerio!' reciprocated Gladys, a wry smile on her face. She wasn't really concerned if John had a skinful - which he would anyway. She didn't begrudge him a little time off. God knows, he worked hard enough in making sure they wanted for nothing. John knew Gladys didn't really disapprove, but still went through with his customary grovelling pretence before any outing.

'Ha way John man!' shouted Roy from the steps of the bus. 'It's time to visit them mills an' t'workhouses in Yorkshire!'

'Get thee pipe man, ar's on me way,' replied John, slamming shut the back door.

He took up a seat at the front of the bus. Customary and compulsory. He was adamant about that right from their first outing. It was only right, him being the landlord and self appointed leader.

'It's alreet for you sitting upfront like lord muck,' carped Roy. 'Yer canna move back 'ere fer the old boy's oxygen bottles an' nebulizers!'

'There'll be plenty o' room in a minute laddo, when I've

chucked you out the back door!' threatened Ronnie.

'Aye, gan on Ron,' Fred encouraged him, 'There'll be more ale fer the rest of us then.'

In a black bin liner, sitting alongside the crates of Brown Ale, was the obligatory blow-up doll. Deflated at the moment, but wouldn't be for long. The doll would soon be placed in a window seat for pedestrians and car passengers alike, to look at in amusement. Did the Weardalers unoriginal humour know no bounds? No doubt, on the journey home, as was customary, Roy would have the unfortunate doll straddled over a seat administering a simulated back scuttle, all egged on by the rampant Phoenix massive. On the otherhand, they could all be paralytic and dead to the world in the land of nod. As on all previous outings, the suspense was unbearable.

'Hold on to your seats gentlemen! Roy as well . . . Leeds, here we come!' heralded Joseph before switching on the ignition to the cheers of the passengers. At eleven-o-eight, the entire cast of 'One Flew Over the Cuckoo's Nest' departed the Phoenix car park, passing as they left, the market cross where John Wesley preached on his seventeenth century tour of the country. Turning onto the main street, Joseph accelerated, destination the A1.

'Yer might 'ave cleaned the bus out Joseph!' shouted Roy down the bus. 'It's filthy man! There's pieces of old kebab meat an' lettuce all ower the floor. Yer've not been on one of yer illegal asylum seeker runs again 'ave yer?'

'Will you stop chelping on?' berated Joseph. 'Ar was up at seven this morning hoovering out Betty (Joseph's pet name for his bus) while you were still festering in yer pit. Though why ar bother I don't know. By the end o' the day, it'll stink o' stale beer, fags an' farts.'

'We pay you a handsome remuneration fer the privilege.'

'It's a tale! You've no idea bonny lad!'

'Ignore him Joseph,' said Dennis. 'Get thee foot down man an' divent spare the horses.'

'You're hoping aren't yer? Top speed's thirty fer this heap.'

'Roy! Give it a rest will yer. Yer getting on everybody's nerves!'

'Okay granda.' Roy stretched out his legs as best he could in the

46

confined space, lay back and closed his eyes.

Stuart, having drawn the short straw and was sitting next to Roy, was already out for the count and snoring like an asthmatic pig.

Arthur, sitting up front alongside John and Joseph, was taking in the panoramic view of the countryside. He was enjoying the invigorating colours, especially the fresh greens this time of year. It must have been a good breeding season, he pondered, noticing the abundance of rabbits dashing for cover at the sound of the approaching minibus. He'd not seen such a mass of rabbits for many a year. Sadly, one thing was certain, the farmers would be working overtime in their endeavours to reduce the numbers. The damage they caused was incalculable.

A peaceful idyll had enveloped the inside of the bus. It seemed as if Joseph had driven through an invisible cloud of lethargy. Even the back of the bus was tranquil. Those not snoozing were reading their chosen tabloid. A few crosswords buffs were engrossed in study, while the gamblers amongst them were checking over horses form, then re-checking before writing out their final selections for the day. In general, the Stanhope massive were re-charging their batteries in readiness for the gruelling schedule which lay ahead. Not least, the copious quantities of alcohol waiting to be consumed. This quiet, reflective period was the calm before the impending storm.

A few lingering clouds were now dispersing. For once, it looked like the weather forecasters had got it it right. Sunny, with a fresh breeze and average temperatures for the time of year. Not that the weather played a major feature in the days activities. It wasn't as if the incorrigible rogues would be laying on a beach all day. They would be warm and dry inside the plentiful public houses at their disposal in Leeds City Centre. Still, whatever was on the agenda, it was still preferable to look out on a bright sunny landscape as opposed to peering through rain spattered windows, which was psychologically depressing no matter what anyone said to the contrary.

'Whey, we've passsed Wolsingham twenty minutes back an' Roy usually 'as that blow-up doll sitting on his lap by now,' remarked Joseph. 'He always gets it out once we're clear o' the local prudes.' Joseph was referring to the insular populace which resided in the vicinity. Every village had their share of moaning Victorian bigots. 'Don't drink, don't smoke, don't swear, don't fart at the dinner table . . . they even get out of the bath fer a piss! When some o' the women 'ave sex, they don't come, they arrive! Their pathetic lives revolve around petty fault finding an' complaining endlessly about everything and everybody. Full of their own importance, their heads stuck firmly up their own arses. What's so ironic is these miserable specimens live on to a ripe old age. Makes you sick doesn't it?'

'Shush . . . Our Roy's dozing,' said Arthur, turning his head back to the front. 'Let sleeping dogs lie while we enjoy the quiet. It's not that often his big mouth's shut. Pass me a tissue an' ar'll wipe up that acid dribbling off 'is tongue down 'is chin.'

John and Joseph quietly laughed, not wanting to wake up the slumbering Roy.

Fred looked up from his newspaper, stretched and yawned. 'Ar see they've not found these weapons o' mass destruction then. According to the honourable Tony Blair, we only had forty-five minutes afore Saddam could release these horrific weapons on the world - God forbid. Yer don't think he was being economical with the truth do yer?'

'Put it this way Frederic,' said John, 'Yer can always tell when Blair's lying - his lips move. He wouldn't know the truth if he stepped ower it.'

'Come on now, be patient chaps, you've got to give the coalition forces time to plant these weapons of Blair's - ar mean - mass destruction,' skitted Joseph. 'Ar nearly said weapons of Blair's imagination then'.

'Hoy lad! We pay a chauffeur to drive, not pass contentious remarks!' berated a tongue-in-cheek Fred.

'I beg your pardon sir.'

'That's okay son. Ar'll let it ride just this once, but think on mind, divent you be getting above your station again - understood?'

'Yes siree. Please forgive me,' said a servile Joseph who was not remotely interested in Iraq - even less with politics, but if it helped pass the time of day, so be it.

"FA Cup" ears Don, was rousing from his slumbers, not sure whether he'd heard his beloved leader being castigated. No, it couldn't be possible could it? Was the transcendent President Blair telepathic? After all, he was the second coming - according to the image reflected from his mirror. 'Were I dreaming or did ar hear our faithful Prime Minister's good name being taken in vain?'

'No, you heard reet Baldrick,' John informed him. 'My God! Quick everybody - look at Don!'

'What is it? What's up?' asked Don, puzzled and bemused.

'Ar can only describe it as . . . radiance . . . a ring of light above your heed . . . encircling you . . . It's absolutely amazing.'

'A ring of light?' asked Don. 'Do yer mean like a halo?'

'No . . . like the Ready Brek advert. It's the son of Blair!'

'More like the son of Ian Duncan-Smith! Yer've got the same hairstyle - or lack of it,' laughed Arthur.

'How original - ar don't think! You may mock our government, but they helped topple that evil dictator!'

'There yer go again Donald, talking aboot Blair,' derided John. 'You're obsessed with him.'

'You nar very well ar was referring to Saddam Hussain.'

'Would that be the same Saddam that's disappeared into thin air? He's probably lying on a tropical island somewhere topping up his tan wi' that Bin-Liner. Counting up his billions an' laughing all the way to the bank. At least that son of 'is was when he loaded up a couple o' lorries wi' bank notes in the middle o' the night. That's what you call irony.'

'He'll be caught. It's just a matter o' time.'

'Oh aye! Like they caught Bin-Liner. All the yanks are interested in is Iraq's oil. That's the first and only thing they secured. All this talk of liberating people is total bollocks. Though they did manage to liberate poor kids from their limbs and murder Iraq's citizens.'

'That's unfortunate. Innocent people do get killed in wars. It's called collateral damage.'

'Well, that's alright then,' skitted an irate John.

'Change the record lads, we're supposed to be on a jolly. Let's get drunk an' enjoy our sens. Leave all that war talk behind.'

'Aye, yer reet Dennis,' agreed Fred, opening a bottle of brown ale. 'Here yer are John, get this down yer neck.'

'Cheers Fred.'

'You're welcome,' said Fred, topping more bottles and handing them around.

Miraculously Roy and Stuart were still asleep. Dennis took his camera from his jacket pocket and crept up to the lads. He carefully placed Stuart's arm around Roy's shoulder. It did cross his mind but would have been more difficult, to put Stuart's hand on Roy's crutch. Giggling like Muttley, Dennis took a photograph. The flash didn't disturb their sleep, or so thought Dennis as he crept away.

Roy had actually been awake a few minutes and had been listening to the chatter. He kept up his pretence another minute while he plotted his revenge.

With his eyes still closed he rose slowly from his seat, bringing his hands together as if in prayer. In a trance-like drawl he spoke, 'The Pearly Gates are prepared O Holy Father. St Peter glosseth over them this morning before breakfast. I must be forth coming and speaketh the truth - though it pains me Heavenly Father. He did foresaketh the undercoat and only useth one coat of Dulux Solo Gloss. It will maketh do as time is short my Father. Hark! Here he is now, o mighty one. 'Tis your son arriveth - the chosen one from Downing Street earth - Blair the Perjurer - Halleluiah!

        All hail to the earth god
        All hail to the Pentagon
        All hail to Downing Street
        All hail to unelected Bush
        All hail to the elected Prick'

Roy continued, 'Breaking news from Iraq has just come in - Six cans of highly inflammable lighter fuel have been discovered, deep beneath a suspiciously large pile of camel shit - More details to follow.'

Billy shook Roy by the shoulders. 'Wake up man!' he bellowed.

'Wh . . . what . . . Where am I?' said Roy, looking round.

'What am I doing aboard this travelling loony bin?' sighed
Joseph before braking sharply and sending Roy into the seat in
front.

'Yer did that on purpose yer great long pillock!'

Joseph had all on to suppress his laughter. 'I'm sorry bonny lad.
Are yer alreet?'

'As if you gived a toss.'

'I'm sorry. Ar had to brake suddenly so ar didn't run over a
ladybird - Me being an animal lover like.'

'Do it again an yer'll get a slap - off Billy.'

'Don't bring me into it,' objected Billy.

'That's blasphemy you've been talking Roy Osborne,' pointed
out Don.

'So? Report me to the Blasphemy Police.'

'You've an answer for everything you. Tony Blair's a Christian
yer nar.'

'Aye, yer reet there Donald,' said John. 'He gans to church once
every four or five years. Coincidentally, the Sunday afore a
general election. Media in tow of course. He could spin fer
England Cricket team that bugger.'

'That's a very cynical view you hold John.'

'With very good reason Don. With very good reason. Ar'll leave
it at that fer now.'

Sighs echoed around the bus and Ronnie jumped in to change
the subject. 'Stuart's still asleep despite all the commotion. D'yer
think he's faking it like Roy?'

'Nar,' stated Alf. 'Ar think 'e must suffer from narcolepsy.'

'What's that when it's at home?' asked Billy.

'It's when someone drops off into a deep sleep wi'out warning.
Must be a nghtmare . . . Hypothetically speaking.'

'Stewpot doesn't 'ave narcolepsy - he's just a lazy pillock.' Roy's
studious expression showed his brain was ticking over. 'Say, Stuart
was boning a bird . . . Highly unlikely ar nar, but for the sake of a
point, just bear with me. Could he be on top of this ugly bird
giving her a good seeing to when all of a sudden he nods off,
pinning her down?'

'Whey, if he suffered from narcolepsy, that's quite possible,'

51

surmised Alf.

'Ar bet he's bust a few bow-up dolls in 'is time then, locked away in 'is bedroom, the dirty little get. That reminds me, pass Muffty ower an' ar'll blow 'er up. Someone else can empty 'er this time - ar've done it the last two times.'

To the shaking of heads and groans of disgust, Roy blew up the doll. He then put it on the floor between Stuart's legs, its face in his crotch. Stuart still slept on.

'Ar wish ar had some o' that squirty cream.'

'Here, yer big kid,' said Fred passing Roy a bottle of brown ale. 'Get this down yer neck.'

'Cheers Frederic.' Roy took a big swig of beer, then placing his thumb over the neck of the bottle, gave it a gentle shake, thus producing frothy bubbles. With a cheesy grin on his face, he spread some of the froth between Stuart's legs and on the doll's face.

Dennis, the unofficial photographer quickly took a picture which would no doubt be passed around the Phoenix clientele the following weekend.

Some of the men were now bursting for the toilet but didn't want to be the first to ask Joseph to stop. They needn't have worried as Roy's comprehensive vocabulary soon surfaced. 'Are yer pulling up soon Joseph - ar's dying fer a piss!'

'Seeing as you so eloquently put it, how can ar resist? Cross yer legs fer five minutes,' said Joseph. 'Ar'll be pulling into Scotch Corner services shortly.'

The relief throughout the bus was palpable. There was always the bucket but that didn't get used until the return journey when full of ale and inhibitions vanished, Joseph had to make frequent stops in the A1 laybys and empty the bucket. Needless to say, he hated the return journey. Everybody pickled out of their heads while he was sober as a judge. Still, he'd make up for it tomorrow. Working every alternate Sunday, tomorrow thankfully, wasn't one of them. He'd go and have a pint - or eight even. These all day opening hours were a godsend, although undoubtably, they'd contributed to many a split relationship or divorce. Following negotiations in the Haynes household, Sunday

52

lunch was put back to four o'clock and John kindly drove Joseph home three-fifty on the the dot every other Sunday.

To say Joseph enjoyed his grub would be an understatement. After a plateful of roast beef dinner that would faze even Desperate Dan, he would get his head down for a few hours blissful sleep. Only occasionally going out on a Sunday night, he and Jean would watch TV or hire a video. He wouldn't be the first person to lose his driving licence and job through a positive breathalyser from the previous nights drinking.

Joseph pulled into Scotch Corner services. 'Right gentlemen! Ten minutes to empty your bladders and anything else that needs emptying. Then we'll mek tracks.'

'Stuart! Hoy!' Roy shook his best mate vigorously, eventually bringing Rip-Van-Winkle back to life.

'What? Are we there?'

'No man, we're at Scotch Corner. Just stopped fer a piss.'

Stuart stretched his body, thus causing the blow up doll to fall off him. 'Bloody hell! Who stuck that there? Forget it, that was a daft question. Aw . . . me kecks are damp! What yer been doing while ar was a kip?'

'How should I nar? Yer must 'ave 'ad a wet dream. Either that or that doll's given yer a blow job,' laughed Roy.

'It's not funny dick head! You're a mentalist you.'

'It has been said.'

'What did yer do, pour ale on me?'

'Yeah, but it was accidental. Yer nar how erratic Joseph's driving is. He braked suddenly, an' a drop of brown ale spilt from from my bottle. Unfortunately, onto your lap. Sorry aboot that Stewpot.'

'Ar bet you are.'

Stuart headed for the toilet, Roy in close pursuit.

Joseph took a thermos flask from a box behind his seat, poured himself a coffee and then reached for a ham and pickle sandwich wrapped in tin foil. He tucked in, enjoying the temporary peace of his empty minibus.

Unlucky Alf, often referred to as Jack Dee because of his dead-pan facial expression climbed aboard the bus. Chuntering away to himself, his face animated - a sign that all was not well with him. 'Ruddy seagulls! How do the flying shit houses nar when yer've put a clean shirt on?'

'Is that why yer've got a wet patch on yer collar Alf?' asked Ronnie.

'Well spotted. Give that man a medal for stating the bleeding obvious. Why they divent stay on the coast is beyond me. Coming inland to bomb respectable citizens going aboot their daily business. Ar swear the one that dumped on me was smirking. They should cull the filthy bastards!'

'Whey, ar knew you were mean skinflint Joseph, but bringing yer own food an' drink teks the biscuit,' skitted John.

'Yer didn't think ar was ganna pay them fancy services prices did yer? Besides, ar've not brought me American Express card with me.'

'Aye. Yer do get ripped off in these places. It's a well known fact,' agreed John.

Unlucky Alf was still dabbing his shirt collar with his handkerchief.

'Never mind Alf, it's supposed to mean good luck,' chortled Fred.

'Bring good luck? Who to? It certainly isn't me!' barked Alf.

Roy was rummaging through Joseph's box of goodies. He held up a bottle of mineral water. 'Hey, ye lot! Listen to what it sez on this label, "This invigorating mineral water has trickled through mountains for centuries. Best used by October 2004."'

Joseph grabbed the bottle from Roy. 'Leave my stuff alone, yer bloody magpie!' Putting it back in his snack box, he did a quick inventory. 'All present and correct, let's hit the road!' he said clicking on his seatbelt. He switched on the ignition and they rejoined the A1.

'Yer wet patch 'as gone then Stuart,' remarked Roy.

'Aye, no thanks to ye. The hand drier shifted it. Be a bit more careful wi' yer booze in future will yer?'

'Okay, divent sweat man. Hey, Fred!'

'Yes son?'

'Lend us yer newspaper will yer?'

Fred handed his paper to Staurt to pass on. 'Divent say ar never give yer nowt. It wouldn't harm you to buy one now an' again.'

'It's against my religion Frederic.'

'Any excuse.'

Roy quickly flicked through the paper in search of any tits and arses on show before settling down to read it. But Roy was unable to read a newspaper in silence, he had to comment on all the articles within.

'Ar see here they've scrapped a fly-on-the-wall documentary aboot that southern nancy boy Vinnie Jones. Trying to copy the Osbornes no doubt. A big mistake. The Osbornes are interesting. They're all mad as hatters. It meks for great telly. Vinnie's boring. Blagged 'is way through life . . . successfully, ar'll give him that like. But hard man? My arse! Ar could tek 'im on wi' one hand tied behind me back.'

'Dream on, Roy,' derided Billy.

'Whey, it's true. Even old Tom'd whoop 'im.'

'Ar divent nar aboot that bonny lad,' said Tom. 'But when yer talk aboot hard men in football, yer've got to gan back a few decades for the real mcCoy.'

'Whey, give us a couple of examples then Tom,' said Arthur, who himself was a bit of a connoisseur in the soccer department.

'Whey, fer instance . . . Chopper Harris - Chelsea. Norman 'bites yer legs' Hunter - Leeds United. Tommy Smith - Liverpool. Oh, an' Billy Bremner, God rest his soul. Ar nearly forgot 'im.'

There was general agreement all round at Tom's choices, but the younger lads couldn't really relate to the aforementioned players, although their reputations went before them and they had had the odd glimpse of them on television.

'In my opinion, yer've been a bit disingenous regards Vinnie Jones,' said Arthur. 'Granted, he was erratic, but when Howard Wilkinson signed him, he must have had a good word with him. Vinnie calmed down and was influential in getting Leeds out of the second division. A leopard can change his spots, ar divent care what they say.'

Arthur, undoubtedly a little biased having a son, daughter-in-law and four grandchildren living in Leeds, always maintained the

Leeds United of the sixties and seventies were the best football team he'd ever seen. 'From Ashington there was Jack 'giraffe neck' Charlton, brother of the famous Bobby. There was Gary Sprake - Leeds and Wales international goalkeeper. He and Charlton didn't get on, always giving each other the verbals during matches. Paul Reaney at right back - he always got the better of George Best. Reaney marked him out of the game everytime they crossed swords. Best was probably pissed in hindsight. There was hotshot Peter Lorimer. He could bust the net if he copped the ball reet. Johnny Giles - the General. A wee fellow who could pass a ball forty yards an' land it on a sixpence - brilliant footballer. An' Billy Bremner . . . the tiger in the tank. A fiery red-headed Scotsman. Hard as nails. Sadly he passed away a couple of years back. There's a statue of him outside Elland Road. He was a local hero. On the left wing there was another Scottish international in Eddie Gray. I forget who Leeds were playing on that day, but ar watched him dribble past six players around the edge of the box afore netting the ball. Another under rated genious. Better than George best in my opinion.'

'That's a bit ower the top Arthur,' said Ronnie in disagreement.

'An' ar'll second that,' said Fred.

But Arthur had an ally in John. 'I agree with you Arthur. Best was brilliant in patches, there's no disputing that. But, over a longer period, I'd 'ave to opt for Eddie Gray. Consistent, reliable. A fantastic footballer who never missed training or a match through booze. As far as I nar anyway.'

Arthur got back on track. 'We had Alan 'Sniffer' Clark upfront. Built like a stick insect, he'd nip between defenders and the ball would be in the back of the net in a flash. There was Paul 'versatile' Madeley. Don Revie could play him in any position . . . and he did. Yer'd think he'd played there all his career. I could go on, but unlike our Roy I wouldn't like to think I was boring you.'

'No way Arthur. It's very interesting,' said Joseph.

Roy, never slow in coming forward got his two pennorth in. 'Leeds United are not so hot these days though are they?' he mocked. 'They only just escaped relegation this season by beating

Arsenal last Sunday. Not exactly 'Super Leeds' any more are they?'

Arthur hit back. 'What's that got to do with owt? I'm not talking aboot these ridiculously overpaid modern day bounty hunters o' today! Thirty an' forty grand a week to play football? It's barmy money man. Ar reckon players should get paid on performance. It might encourage some o' the lazy ones to put some effort into their game then. A rocket up their backside now an' again wouldn't gan amiss either. This present team aren't fit to lace the boots of the past master Leeds United players.'

'Ar think you're being a bit harsh Arthur,' said Fred. 'Leeds sold a lot of their top players this last season. World class ones at that. Rio Ferdinand to Man United, Robbie Fowler to Man City - though 'e did nowt fer the team. Lee Bowyer to West ham. Admitted, his reputation wasn't the best, but he gave a hundred percent for Leeds. An' selling Woodgate to Newcastle - a young world class player, could be the straw that breks the camel's back.'

'Fair enough Fred, but the players left at Elland Road are supposedly the best in the Premiership. Paul Robinson, Danny Mills, Ian Harte, Gary Kelly, young Alan Smith, not least Mark Viduka. An' one of the best footballers in the country, if not the world - Harry Kewell. The trouble is, Leeds are heavily in debt, so who nars what players'll be left, come the new season.'

'How come you're so genned up on Leeds United Arthur?' asked Stuart.

'Ar used to go an' watch 'em with our Johnny. He only lives aboot three mile from the ground on Bramley Ring Road. I'd travel down once a month, sometimes fortnightly to watch 'em play. After the match we'd go back to our Johnny's fer a spot of tea an' then it was down to 'is local club come evening. I'd stay overneet an' travel back home Sunday morning. Happy days bonny lad, happy days.'

'Are yer meeting up wi' your Johnny today Arthur?'

'Nar, he's gone off on holiday to Spain with 'is next door neighbour Stan. Lucky buggers. Ar wish ar was with 'em. He rang me up last week - says he'll be in Stanhope in aboot a month. He recommended a book an' video aboot the Famous Super Leeds team. It's on sale in Borders bookstore in Briggate. Ar'll 'ave a gander an' most likely buy 'em.'

'Borders? Ar've never heard o' them,' said Stuart. 'Yer might get 'em cheaper from WH Smith or Waterstones,' he pointed out.

'Borders are an American store apparently - fairly new to Britain. Ar canna be bothered comparing prices. Besides, most o' the book shops are priced the same across the board.'

'Yer should ask our Alistair granda,' said Roy. 'He's a reet bookworm. He'll nar the price of every book on sale in Leeds. He's a walking encyclopedia 'imself.'

'Yer might be reet Roy. Ar'll 'ave word with 'im afore buying owt. All o' the press were anti Leeds yer nar,' reflected Arthur. 'Probably because all the London football teams were shite - like their newspapers. In the old days yer could stand up to watch the game an' all. It made fer a better atmosphere. This compulsory seating is a waste of time. Every bugger in front of yer keeps standing up an' obscuring yer view. I'm glad we had the golden years afore money was God. Football ceased to be a sport years ago. It's big business nowadays. Ar divent nar how the ordinary working man - if there is such a thing nowadays - can afford to gan to a match.'

'It says here,' said Roy looking up from his paper, 'Newcastle United's trophy room was broken into yesterday. Police are looking for a bloke carrying a green carpet,' he chuckled.

This brought jeers from eight of the group who were avid supporters of Newcastle.

'One word Royston,' said Fred. 'No, I tell a lie - two words. Sunderland . . . Relegation.'

This time cheers ensued.

'Doesn't bother me one iota,' said Roy trying to appear nonchalant. 'I am now a supporter of the Premiership champions. Having seen the error of my ways in following that bag o' shite Sunderland, ar's now Man United's number one fan.'

'Bloody turncoat,' sneered Billy.

'Aye. Fair weather supporter,' added Stuart.

Both he and Billy were loyal supporters of Newcastle. Football in the north east was a way of life and it would not be an exaggeration in saying they lived for the game. A recent study had shown Sunderland supporters had twice the average hypertension and other stress related illness while watching their team play at home. Bill Shankly wasn't far off the mark when he said, 'Football's not just a matter of life and death, it's far more important than that.'

Chapter 4

Roy looked up from the TV magazine he was reading. 'Bah . . . television's a load o' rubbish lately. It's nearly all women's programmes. Changing wombs . . . Call by Muff . . .'

Groans and sighs echoed around the bus. Roy, undeterred, carried on. 'Wait, there's more. Through the Pee-Hole . . . 'Can't Cook, Won't Fook . . . Come Dancing. Then there's that crap Bargain C. . . runt. Whoops! nearly swore then. A seventy year old Tango man salivating ower a bit of old tat that Steptoe an' Son'd reject. What's it all coming to . . . I ask yer. It's enough to drive a man to drink.'

'An' it does. Unfortunately to my pub,' muttered John.

Ronnie was reading a magazine and had come across a satirical account of a man's visit to a hospital which he read with amusement. Quote:- I was in an accident recently which unfortunately left me in an unconscious state and I awoke to find myself laid out prostrate on a trolley. In my confusion I swore that I was deposited in an Asda Superstore, until a kindly gentleman in a blue overall pointed out to me that I was actually in the corridor of a midland's hospital. Still dazed and nodding off fitfully, I was soon brought back to reality with a bang when I inadvertently fell off the trolley whilst rolling over in search of a more comfortable position. Luckily for me, the thick layer of dust on the floor substantially cushioned my fall. Unfazed, staff later explained to me how fortunate I was in being allocated a trolley, even one without a safety rail. Apparently, all the superior trolleys had been occupied some days earlier. Luck of the draw I suppose, but I was comfortingly assured another ten new trolleys - 'in real terms' - had been ordered for the year 2010.

I lay there bored but not unduly concerned as I surveyed the flaking ceiling paint. I was quite impressed with the Spiderman like skills Kilroy must possess to climb such heights just to leave his signature on a ceiling for patients to peruse. How thoughtful in this day of all me, me, me. It gives one hope doesn't it?

The filthy state of the hospital didn't unduly concern me. After all, that nice Mr Blair and his cronies, sorry - ministers - have promised to send in 'hit squads' to deal with this irritation - I mean situation - over the next ten years. There you go see? Tough on grime, tough on causes of grime. Up to date no one has seen these elusive 'hit squads' but we must not despair. Maybe they're invisible, like the Iraqi weapons of destruction. Who knows?

People should stop all this whinging and criticising of our beloved NHS. Just because they have to wait a couple of years to see a consultant . . . dragging him away from his private practice. It's a disgrace man. After all, they're the ones who made themselves ill. Fancy . . . eating contaminated meat . . . GM foodstuffs (granted, they're hidden) fruit and veg saturated with pesticides. £1.20 chickens riddled with salmonella. I've no sympathy with them whatsoever. All this pestering to be seen within five or six years must stop instantly. Don't they realise the pressure this puts on the hospital administrators? Selfish. No other word for it. A modern future National Health Service should be embraced (as if) by these doom and gloom merchants. Besides, most patients will be dead before getting any medical treatment. Problem solved - No worries then. Hypochondriacs the lot of them. Don't these people read newspapers or listen to the news? Labour has promised 20,000 new refugees - sorry, I mean student nurses - over the next fifteeen years, to run wards on their own. Another manifesto pledge honoured. Patients may moan, but look - They've stuck to their pledge like shit to a blanket. Quite appropriate in this place, don't you think?

The thought of all this extra care to come kept my spirits up, although, as I checked my watch it dawned on me that no one had attended my injuries after sixteen hours. Still, Rome wasn't built in a day. Give Tony a chance. Eighteen years of Tory neglect can't be overturned in six short years you know. It'll take time. Be a patient patient.

Eighteen hours . . . I think I'll play I Spy . . . No hold on, there's a little foreign chap approaching my trolley. What did I tell you? I'm next to be seen. Service second to none.

My ecstasy short lived. Slightly disappointed, it was a bloke selling raffle tickets. I admit, I purchased one, but how could any normal, rational thinking person resist when the first prize was an overnight stay in a real bed on a designated ward. I was sorely tempted to buy another ticket when I discovered the second prize was a pillow complete with unstained pillow case. Alas, my funds didn't stretch to it.

Two hours later

Good news! I won first prize in the raffle. A bed for the night. There is a God. "Just give us half an hour or so Mr Lister" I was told."While we get rid of this ninety year old, mallingering bed blocking bastard. Two weeks the old git's occupied that bed. Flu my arse. Thankfully his relations have managed to sell off his house. Doctor Rasheed's cousin has kindly found him a broom cupboard in one of his nice private nursing homes. Only £800 a week too. What would we do without our kindly ethnic friends? It doesn't bear thinking about does it? They don't know they're born our old folk and that's a fact, Mr Rasheed's cousin has even offered to take care of the old boy's £200 heating allowance - Just until he's right in the head like. How kind is that I ask you?"

At least my grandfather isn't bothered with all that hospital bed and waiting list shite. The kind Mr Blair says that he can be cared for at home in his own comfortable bed, which means he won't be counted as one of those pests causing waiting lists to grow. In fact, on account of my grandfather being a schizophrenic - that's two less on that burdensome list of ungrateful old imbeciles.

Hey up! Here comes a nice little sixteen year old Philippino nurse to escort me to my winning bed. Yippee!

Had an early night. Asleep by ten thirty. I didn't have any two pound coins for the television slot meter. Not a bad night's kip overall - apart from the odd noise interruption. Between you and me, I think some of these foreign nurses are a bit sadistic. I was woken a few times through the night by men moaning and groaning.

It's mid morning - mildly disappointed - I've not had a cuppa yet. I enquired of a fellow patient what time the tea-lady did her rounds and was informed, somewhat to my astonishment, that the service was no more. Apparently, the tea trolley had been commandeered for use as a bunk bed in the children's ward.

11o'clock and I'm being examined by a junior accountant - sorry, I mean doctor. He has massive bags under his eyes and tells me he's only slept twenty minutes in the last three days. I told him to stop complaining. Doesn't he know he'll get thirty minutes in the year 2012? Always whinging these young ones of today. If they'd worked down t'pit eighteen hours a day without a break, eight days a week, they'd know about it.

11.30 A little Philippino nurse is pulling the curtains round me. Must me my turn for some light relief. Things are looking up.

Footnote:- Foundation hospitals are on the horizon - Funny, I thought they'd already hit rock bottom - c/o New Labour - Silly me.

Finishing the tale, Ronnie allowed himself a sardonic smile.

'Yer've made good time Jo lad,' said Arthur, noticing the sign for Wetherby. 'It's barely half past twelve an' we had that toilet stop at Scotch Corner.'

'Aye well, we've had a straight run Arthur. No accident black spots or other hold ups. Twenty-five or thirty minutes an' we'll be in Leeds - touch wood,' said Joseph, jokingly tapping John's forehead.

'Hey! Watch it son! There's nowt but brains up there.'

'Thought we must be nearing Leeds, ar can smell the fumes,' said Roy. 'There might be nowt to dee in Stanhope but at least yer can breathe fresh air.'

'Not if yer stood next to you in the pub,' skitted Stuart.

'Roy does 'ave a point though,' stated Dennis. 'Come next year, motorists'll be charged five pund to drive through Leeds. An' many other cities'll follow no doubt. Eeh . . . paying a toll for the privilege of sitting in traffic jams. That's the governments answer to everything. Picking ower pockets at every turn. According to them we should leave our cars at home an' use the the fantastic public transport. The fact that it barely exists seems to escaped their notice - or has it? Truth be known, the more vehicles gridlocked on our roads, spewing out fumes, the better for them. All that fuel duty filling the coffers an' now more taxes fer having the cheek to drive on the road. Ar thought that was why we paid road tax. Ar bet the treasury canna count the brass quick enough. Daylight bloody robbery.'

'Yer not wrong Dennis. It's a disgrace,' agreed Joseph.

Roy, bored with the subject matter, turned his attention elsewhere. 'Whey, yer can tell we're in Yorkshire, all the sheep are wearing flat caps. The farmers divent use sheepdogs to round 'em up, but whippets. We'll soon be coming to the Yorkshire Pudding factories. Can't yer pass this tin can Joseph?' he said, referring to a caravan in front. 'We'll never get there stuck behind that at twenty mile an hour.'

'Divent try teach yer grandmother how to suck eggs,' was Joseph's response.

'Ar divent. She nars how to do it. She just leaves her false teeth out.'

'Just ower this bridge on the river Wharfe an' we've reached the end of the motorway,' Joseph informed them.

'Hey up!' exclaimed John, 'There's Tony Blair ower there, walking on the river!'

'Divent talk so daft man. Why would he be walking on the river when 'e can fly ower it?' said Dennis.

'It's alright ye lot mocking Tony Blair. He's the finest Prime Minister this county's ever had,' defended Don, a staunch fully paid up member of the so called 'New Labour Party' - one of a rapidly declining number. 'Ar divent hear any of you old boys complaining aboot the two hundred pund fuel allowance this government generously brought in.'

'What do they need a fuel allowance for?' said Roy. 'It's just extra beer money paid for out o' my taxes. They're always on the piss, keeping warm in the Phoenix or down the club. Mind . . .

that depends on whether John's in a charitable mood whether the heating's on in the Phoenix.'

'Whey, if yer not happy aboot it, complain to the government,' suggested old Tom.

'Better still Roy, why not become an MP and help change the policy,' added Frank.

'Good idea Frank, Roy's always been a great mass . . . debater.'

'He's always been a wanker is what yer trying to say Tom,' said Billy.

'Spot on young en.'

'Bollocks,' was Roy's response.

'Not that he'd ever be elected if he stood,' said Ronnie. 'Have you got a police record Roy?'

'Aye, 'Walking on the Moon'! spat out Roy.

'The old ones are the best,' smiled Billy.

'We're in Percy Shaw country now chaps,' remarked Joseph.

'These young ens winna nar who yer on aboot man,' said Arthur.

'That's nee problem. I shall educate them . . . Percy Shaw invented the Catseye. He was a Halifax mill owner in the first half of the last century. One dark winter's night, driving home from the pub, on rounding a sharp bend in the road his car headlights reflected in a pair of cat's eyes. This gave him the idea which resulted in the brilliant invention of the springy reflective Catseyes in the middle of our roads. Needless to say, it made him a fortune.'

'That's very interesting driver - Not,' skitted Roy. 'Hang on a minute though . . . Does that mean that if the cat in question had been walking the other way, he'd 'ave invented the pencil sharpener?'

Laughter throughout the bus followed and in a jovial mood the party broke into song.

Dance to your daddy, my little laddie
Dance to your daddy, my little one.
You shall have a fishy on a little dishy
You shall have a fishy when the boat come.

Stuart, unimpressed stuck his fingers in his ears. 'Ar think ar'd rather listen to Roy than the cat's choir!' he shouted in Billy's ear-hole.

'Ar wouldn't gan that far!' shouted Billy in return. 'All we need now is ower Alistair strangling a rendition of On Ilkley Moor Ba'tad, or whatever it is.'

'Divent speak too soon. We've got 'im aboard on the way home, remember?'

'Aye, yer reet Stewpot. Ar'd forgotten fer a minute there. It winna matter though, cos by then ar'll be pissed as a fart, like everbody else nee doubt.'

'Oppen yer window will yer Joseph? It stinks bloody awful back 'ere man!' shouted Roy. 'Has one of ye old boy's colostomy bags got a leak or what?'

'There's none of us got a colostomy bag, yer gobshite. It'll be your nose that's too close to yer arse,' skitted old Tom.

Ignoring Tom's remark, Roy cleared his throat. 'Reet - my turn to sing.'

Sighs of resignation reverberated within.

'Feel free to join in at any time. Here we gan then, one two three:-

> It was on the bridge at midnight
> Picking clinkers from her crutch.
> She said she'd never had it,
> I said, not bloody much.
> It's the same the whole world over
> Ain't it all a ruddy shame
> It's the rich that gets the gravy
> And the poor that gets the blame.'

'Brings a tear to yer eye,' said Fred.

'It's the poet laureate,' skitted Ronnie. 'Yer've missed yer calling Royston. He's certainly got a way wi' words 'as your grandson o' yours Arthur.'

Arthur tutted, shaking his head. 'Hasn't he just.'

'Whey, thank you very much gentlemen,' said Roy, standing up and taking a bow. 'There's more where that came from, seeing as it went down so well. This is a bit more refined like . . . Are you all sitting comfortably? Then I'll begin:-

> Shall I compare thee to a summer's day

Thou art more lovely than . . . '

'Shut up!' shouted everyone in unison.

'Alreet, alreet, keep yer 'air on! Them that's got any. Yer miserable set o' sods. Pass us a bottle o' bown ale please Fred.'

Removing the top first, Fred passed Roy a bottle. Roy thanked him, and then gulped down a large swig. 'This broon ale's manky John. It tastes stale. 'Ow old is it?'

'Whey check the date an' yer'll find out,' suggested John.

Roy examined the label. 'Ar canna tell, the months 'ave been scratched off man.'

'Whey, that'll be the mice in the cellar then, the little buggers, but divent you worry bonny lad, the ale's not out o' date.'

'Yer'll tell me owt. Ar'll believe yer where thousands wouldn't,' muttered Roy before taking another big gulp, proving the quality of the beer despite his protestations. 'Where we meeting up with ower Alistair again? Jog me memory will yer?'

'Whitelocks on Briggate,' obliged Stuart.

'Why aye, o' course. Ar remember. It wouldn't 'ave surprised me if he hadn't arranged to meet up in Leeds Central Library. The skinny Yorkshire puff thinks he's some kind of academic, ganning on aboot politics an' shite like that. It's not reet, a lad of his age. Oh, an' did yer nar he's writing a book now in 'is spare time? What a pillock! I ask you. He wants to get on a building site an' do some proper work. Mind you, he's got a degree in boredom, ar'll give 'im that.'

'You're only jealous cos he talks sense as opposed to your constant bullshit,' skitted Stuart.

'Bollocks! I'm a man of the world bonny lad.'

'Aye, but which world? In which universe?'

'It'd be nice to 'ave a library,' remarked old Tom. 'Granted, there's the mobile library parks up at the Dales Centre once a week, but it comes during pub hours. That's nee good to the likes of us. Do yer nar . . . ?We had better services In Stanhope fifty years ago.'

'Yer not wrong Tom,' said Fred. 'We've nee bookies either. A couple more years an' we'll be living in a ghost town. It's only a matter o' time afore they shut the Post Office down as well. The government's forcing us to 'ave ower pensions paid into a bank account. An' if yer bank's shut down like in some villages - yer up shit creek.'

Why divent yer get on-line like me then? I'd be lost without the internet,' enthused Don. 'On-line banking . . . chat rooms etc. It's brilliant.'

'Yeah, he's reet. Yer can tap into some great porn sites,' smirked Roy.

'Trust you.'

'We're too old to start all that computer stuff even if we wanted to,' said Tom resignedly.

'You're never too old,' insisted Don.

'Wait up a minute, rewind a bit. What was all that aboot pensions Fred?' asked an anxious looking Alf.

Fred went on to explain. 'Over the next few months the benefits agency are gonna be writing to you asking fer yer bank account details - that's assuming you've got one like. Once yer've given it to them, yer've given up yer right to collect yer pension at the Post Office. Hence, the government will cut back on monies paid to the Post Office for handling fees an' cause loads of 'em to shut down. Apparently, yer can open up an account there if you want to, and yer'll be given a pin number for withdrawals.'

'Obviously, wi' this lot running the country, it winna be that simple,' pointed out Ronnie. 'Our kid, who lives down south as yer nar, says yer've got to jump through hoops to get yer money paid at the Post Office. He says you 'ave to phone up constantly to get one o' these 'Invitation forms.' Basically, they just mess you about. When you think on it, it's all typical New Labour harassing people who canna fight back - the old, the sick an' the disabled. An' the unemployed as well. All this while they're sucking up to big business fraudsters - money fer favours.'

'That's a bit strong,' remonstrated Don. 'Labour's only trying to cut down on benefit fraud.'

'Rubbish,' replied Fred.

'Hey up,' whispered Roy. 'Not the conspiracy theory again.'

'It's big brother,' mused Alf. 'The buggers want to nar how much yer've got in the bank.'

'Divent look so worried Alfred man,' said Tom, reassuringly patting Alf on the back. 'Yer'll not starve to death. It'll all sort itself out one way or another.'

'Anyway, stop yer moaning Alf old boy,' said Roy. 'Ar have it on good authority yer've got a couple o' grand tucked away under yer mattress,' teased Roy in an attempt to lighten what he considered a monotonous discussion.

'That's an out an' out lie! Retract that statement immediately Royston Osborne - It's hidden in a biscuit tin!' smirked Alf.

'Look! Another McDonald's ower there,' pointed out Roy. 'I remember him when he only had a farm.'

'Beam me up Scottie, ar canna tek no more,' sighed Billy. 'Pass me another bottle Fred.'

'Whey, we're nearly there now, is it worth oppening another?' asked Joseph as he competently negotiated a busy roundabout.

'Nee problem. Stuart'll help me down it won't yer?'

'It'll be my pleasure.'

Fred topped a bottle and handed it to Billy. 'Anyone else while I'm at it? There's ten brown ale an' one an' a half bottles of whiskey.'

Everyone declined Fred's offer, most of them bloated and in need of emptying their bladders once again.

'We'll see off the rest on the way home,' said John. 'We've a long day ahead.'

'Arthur an' Dennis'll see to that, nee danger,' skitted Frank.

'Never a truer word bonny lad. Never a truer word,' confirmed Arthur.

Ralph Paynel inherited Leeds around 1200. He discovered that his family had already given away the main village, leaving him with very little income. To solve this dilemma, he established a very large 'new town' in 1207. This comprised of a huge central market area with thirty plots for houses, shops and gardens extending on both sides to back lanes. This market place later became known as Briggate. Bryeg, being the old English word for bridge and gata, the old Norse name for a way or street.

Parking up adjacent to Kirkgate Market, the Weardalers leapt from the minibus - with a few exception of course - and made straight for the gents toilets in the bus station. So desperate were they to relieve themselves of Scottish and Newcastle Brewery's finest.

Joseph quickly gave his bus the once over. Laying Muffty on the floor, he locked up for the day and headed toward the gents. As he passed the police station he saw a dozen or so community officers coming out. The governments latest ploy. Anything but properly trained police officers. 'Policing on the cheap,' muttered Joseph, thinking to himself as he continued on his way that these new tax collectors would soon be given the powers to fine people on the spot (once the white paper had been rushed through the House of Commons) for such serious misdemeanours as dropping litter or cigarettes, dog fouling or worse still . . . standing on the the cracks between pavements. More money to fill the coffers from the people who can least afford it - never mind the violent street muggers. There's no money in trying to apprehend the country's scum. This was the present reality and it could only get worse. 'Great Britain,' - if only. It's a bloody frightening war zone out there.

Not unfamiliar with the Leeds area, having lived there for a few years in the eighties. Joseph had moved down from Stanhope and rented a small flat while he was driving buses for Leeds City Transport. Becoming homesick, he returned to his native village in the summer of 1987 after securing a driving job via his father with Weardale United Bus Services. A much more sedate vocation he soon came to realise. Travelling through the beautiful Weardale countryside as opposed to the hustle and bustle rat race of Leeds. Alright for the indigenous populace but a bit much, after a while for a country bumpkin.

Sitting on a bench beside the public conveniences, Joseph awarded himself a wry smile. He observed old Tom coming out, wiping his hands down his black cotton drill trousers - presumably drying them off. How deceptive a person's appearance can be, pondered Joseph. Whoever uttered the saying 'never judge a book by its cover' certainly knew their onions. Tom, at 74 and five foot two inches tall if you were generous, was a wiry Albert Steptoe look-a-like with an amazing capacity for drinking copious amounts of alcohol. Indeed, his constitution would baffle the finest doctors money could buy. You'd find the cheery old rascal just a tad more convivial than the norm after a dozen pints of ale, occasionally followed by whiskey chasers, but nobody could honestly recall ever seeing the popular little character any the worse for wear. The man was a human sponge with an indestructible liver, which was incredible considering he was barely eight and a half stone wet through.

Joseph began mentally counting to ten in his head. Sure enough, he'd hardly reached six when, right on cue the other three old old boys emerged. They might as well be joined at the hip, which some folks (namely Roy) maintained they already were.

'Bloody typical Yorkshire stinginess,' grumbled Fred, rubbing his hands together. 'Nee paper towels an' the hand driers divent work. It's worse than the bloody Phoenix.'

'Wasn't there any bog roll?' asked Joseph.

'Ar wouldn't nar. All the cubicles were engaged. It stinks to bloody high heaven in there. There's some serious waste disposal ganning on, ar can tell yer.'

Within five minutes most of the clan were gathered together, leaving only the court jester to complete the group. Roy soon turned up, preceded by his loud mouth before he even came into view.

'Yer canna have a shite in peace these days. What's it coming to?'

'What's up now?' sighed Billy.

'Oh, an' by the way, the mystery is over,' announced Roy. 'Ar've found the weapons of mass destruction. They were in my underpants!'

'Dream on,' sneered Billy. 'What was it yer were moaning on aboot anyway?'

'Whey, ar was sat on the crapper, as yer do, getting rid of John's sour ale . . . '

'Was there any bog paper?' interrupted Fred.

'Yeah, why? There was any amount. Anyway, back to my tale.

As I was saying . . . Ar was sat having a dump when the bloke in the next cubicle kept groaning as if in some considerable amount of discomfort. Being the caring individual that I am, ar was aboot to enquire after the poor fellows health, when ar came to my senses. Remembering where I was, it dawned on me that it must 'ave been a Yorkshireman in agony. So tight, that 'e didn't want to part with his own shit!'

'You're a rotten git. The poor bloke's probably constipated.'
'Aye, yer might be reet Stewpot. He'll be bunged up wi' Yorkshire Puddings! A pint o' John's mouldy old ale'll soon get him shifted.'

'Reet, that's ye barred from my pub,' declared John.

'Give ower man, it's me that keeps the place ganning. Not least, all that extra trade yer benefit from my presence.'

'Oh aye,' scoffed John. 'An' pray tell, what extra trade might that be? I'm dying to nar.'

'Whey, all them lovely young ladies I attract.'

'Slappers more like,' muttered Billy.

'An' think on, mine host, these birds of today sup pints. None of yer half pint measures - having said that, the collar you leave on a pint meks it nearer threequarters - but that's another matter. Back to the plot . . . Some of 'em can drink the men under the table. An' it gans wi'out saying - ar hasten to add, ar divent include myself wi' them wimps.'

'When I come to think of it - ar've got a pub full of piss artists,' mused John.

'Hey, divent knock it. Other pubs in Stanhope are struggling, like thousands throughout the land. They'd kill fer your trade man. In fact, it must be said, ar canna gan on living a lie - as most of your custom is mainly down to my goodself frequenting your premises, this is where ar take issue with you . . . Ar bring so much to the table, clientele wise, I find it highly offensive in having to pay fer my beer. Have you no guilt man? An' ar think yer'll find the chaps back me up on this one.'

'No we divent!' came the resounding renunciation.'

'Like that is it? So much for loyalty between life-long friends. Typical - All for one and one for one is the modern day cancer of selfishness that blights throughout our society. Alas! There's no hope.'

'What the hell are you rambling on aboot? Yer big girl's blouse,' derided Stuart. 'Have yer been popping them pills again?'

'An' what pills might them be?' asked Roy's stern looking grandad.

'No need to fret Arthur. It was just a meaningless wise crack,' said Stuart, hoping he'd reassured Arthur.

'Good. He's bad enough with alcohol. God forbid if he took any more stimulants.'

'Yer've nee worries on that score granda. High on life - that's me,' stated Roy. 'Contrary to many misguided beliefs, ar do have a brain. Drugs are for losers.'

'So yer do tek 'em,' goaded Billy.

'Very funny, yer ginger twat. Yer nar exactly what are mean.'

'Alright, settle down. Just a joke. I divent bother wi' drugs either but ar nar plenty who do. It's rife everywhere man, even in schools. Mind you, the government mek it worse, muddying the waters. If the police find a certain amount of marijuana on you, yer okay, but a larger amount an' they can arrest you as a dealer. What they need is a decent debate - out in the open. Amsterdam 'ave got it sorted with their marijuana cafes. Folks nar where they stand.'

'Aye, it's all flat ower there so they all ride bikes. That's why they smoke grass, so they can imagine the scenery as they ride along,' said Roy, tongue firmly in cheek.

'Trust you to come out wi' summat like that. What about crack then?'

'Oh, stuff that. Leave it to the puffs.'

'Not that sort of crack! Oh, I give in. You're just tekking the piss.'

'Whey, you started it.'

'If ar could just jump in here children, while I think on,' interrupted Stuart. 'On a more serious note fer a moment . . . Never leave your drink unattended. I've read aboot these city pubs. There's perverts all ower the place. When they've singled someone out, they wait while they're not looking - gone to the toilet or summat, an' pop gorilla tranquillisers into their drink.

74

Next thing, they nar is waking up in a strange place, handcuffed to a bed an' sore as hell after being rodgered all night.'

'Give ower Stewpot, I'm getting a semi on,' said Roy.

'No surprise there then. The only time you get to touch up a bird is when yer've spilled a drink down her an' she's comatosed.'

'Bollocks! You're just jealous of my prowess in the trouser department.'

'Ar thought it were just the lasses that had to worry aboot someone spiking their drinks,' said Billy.

'That's where yer wrong bonny lad. Homosexuals can just as easily slip a sedative in yer pint, so be alert.'

'Ar tell yer this much,' said an animated Roy. 'If anyone so much as comes near my arse, ar'll deck 'em on the spot. Ar may reluctantly tolerate puffs, being a modern man like - so long as they stick to own kind there's nee problem. I'm strictly a beaver man meself an' always will be.'

'Well, I'm sure the homosexual community'll be relieved to here that,' said Stuart. 'People are who they are. End of story.'

'Yeah, okay, I get your point, but it doesn't mean ar'll ever get my heed round this brown love lark. They must walk aboot like John Wayne. Their arse permanently sore.'

'Theoretically speaking,' chipped in Billy. 'If, for whatever reason I was a shirt-lifter - which is not gonna happen ar might add - I'd 'ave to be a giver, not a receiver. Stuff that fer a lark,' he grimaced. 'No pun intended like.'

'Anyway Roy,' said Stuart, 'Ar divent nar why you've got such strong views on the subject, when the only requisite a bird needs to gan out with you is a pulse an' several orifices!'

'That's very funny, Milky Bar Kid. My insides are aching.' With that, Roy strolled off to investigate some market stalls, returning a couple of minutes later wearing a flat cap.

'Hey up, it's Andy Capp!' laughed Billy.

'When in Rome . . . Only £2.99 an' all!' said a grinning Roy.

'Those were the days when pubs an' clubs had 'men only' rooms,' cogitated Ronnie.

Stanhope working men's club's 'men only' room had become a

mixed area of recent years and this had not gone down too well with the majority of male members.

'We could air our views in privacy . . . not watch ower language. Aye . . . happy days.'

'Yer reet there Ron,' agreed Unlucky Alf.

John failed to back them up because he personlly preferred the mixed pubs and clubs. He was equally at home conversing with both sexes. Most women these days worked full-time or part-time. Long gone were the days when only the husband went out to work while the wife stayed home with only the one wage coming in. Good riddance to 'the good old days.' As far as he was concerned, they were just a myth.

'Ar tell yer what, if I ever get hitched our lass'll stay at home an' do the cooking an' cleaning, washing an' ironing . . . shopping an' decorating an' gardening. No wife of mine's working,' said Roy, an inane grin breaking out across his face.

'Yer get dafter by the day,' laughed John.

'Seriously though, ar couldn't imagine a pub wi' no lasses. Thank God fer them suffering gets . . . that Emily Plankhurst an' fellow lesbians pushing forward slapper's rights.'

'You're all heart Royston.'

'That's me.'

Joseph was studying Quarry Hill opposite the bus station. Sited there, in the eastern part of the city was the colossal DSS building known locally as 'The Kremlin' so named because of its likeness to its Russian counterpart. It had opened some years earlier with more than a little hostility due to its opulence. Amongst other things, an indoor swimming pool, expensive paintings and thick luxurious carpets. Costing a fortune, at the tax-payers expense, it was regarded as a totally unnecessary waste of money by the vast majority of Leeds residents. Far better to have spent the capitol on the needy and entitled, than pampering DSS employees with lavish furnishings and fittings.

Years earlier at Quarry Hill, Leeds Corporation had created a compound of dwellings that was Utopian in its day, being reputed throughout Europe as a fundamental approach to re-housing. The first development was opened in 1938, allowing Leeds

Corporation to provide accommodation for more than 3000 people. The concrete structures ranged from four to eight storeys and were sited over more more than 23 acres of land. There were 938 flats in total, the upper ones reached by lifts. An innovative rubbish disposal system was installed. With water heated from the central incinerator, laundry facilities were accessible. Playgrounds were provided for the children and shops and a Post Office were on hand.

Hitler had planned to utilize the massive complex as his SS Headquarters after defeating Britain.

Quarry Hill flats were completely demolished by 1978.

Chapter 5

'Right, we're all present an' correct - sort of. So, are we all ready for the off?' asked Joseph. 'Seeing as ar's familiar with the area, ar'll be navigator. We'll cut across the market here, an' then go through the indoor one. Across Vicar Lane and through the prestigious Victoria Quarter to Briggate.'

'Lead the way then Marco Polo,' said Arthur sarcastically. 'Some of us 'ave been to Leeds afore yer nar.'

'Ar never said yer hadn't. Just trying to be helpful that's all,' pointed out Joseph, somewhat miffed.

'Fair enough, divent tek umbrage bonny lad. Go Forth.'

To the shouts of the fruit and vegetable sellers plying their wares, the Weardalers made their way through the dozens of stalls covering the large outdoor market area.

'Get yer bananas! Only 20p a pound!' Then the wag added, 'Make that 20p a half kilo! Don't want the politically correct police carting me off to the dungeon!'

Another shouted, 'Get yer bananas here! All with their natural curves! But hurry, hurry, hurry afore Brussels mek 'em illegal!'

This was countered by the vendor opposite shouting, 'Get your orders in now! Coming soon, straight bananas this autumn! A free oblong fruit bowl for the first twenty customers!'

And, so it went on. The punters loved the patter and the sellers enjoyed the crack. It made the working day go much faster and upped their profits. Standing silent behind a stall didn't earn you much money, so it was not a job for introverts.

There was a Del Boy at every turn. You name it, you could buy

it. Books, videos, CDs, vinyl records, tools, bric-a-brac, clothes . . .
Pirate goods wouldn't be hard to find either. They went hand in
hand with markets as much as they did in pubs and car boot sales.
You paid your money and took your chance - no guarantees - As
in the 90s advertisement of a young lad returning a very inferior
pirate video tape to a Del Boy, 'Verbal agreement mate. There
was no trains in 'Trainspotting' neither!' the wide boy bellowed to
the unfortunate retreating victim.

'That smells grand,' said Stuart, closing his eyes, taking in the
aroma of fried onions, simmering hotdogs and burgers.

'Aye, yer reet,' said Roy. 'Ar think ar'll partake of a mucky
burger wi' onions.'

'Count me in an' all,' said Billy.

'Yer not having a meal with us in Whitelocks then?' asked
Dennis.

'Nar,' dismissed Roy. 'There'll be less room fer ale man. A nice
greasy burger'll suffice. We'll leave the sit down meal jobs to ye
old folks. An' divent be running to me wi' Yorkshire Pudding
poisoning neither.'

'Whey, I think ar'd be more inclined to worry aboot what a
beefburger consisted of these days. I'm happy placing my faith in
a batter mix, thank you very much.'

'Get a mucky burger down yer Dennis man! Live dangerous fer
once.'

'Pass. Ar'll leave that junk food to ye young ens.'

As the lads purchased their 'Russian Roulette' in a bread bun,
the rest of the party browsed around the plethora of market stalls.

Kirkgate Market stands on the site of the medieval Vicar's
Croft. The pig, cattle, and fruit and vegetable markets were
relocated here from Briggate in 1882. Between 1991 and 1993 it
was completely refurbished to it's original magnificence by the
City Council in coalition with Norwich Union. The interior, with
it's fine cast iron framing is decorated with the City Arms in it's
arches. Red dragons below it's balconies and primary cast iron
market stalls. The clock beneath the central dome was presented
by Marks and Spencer to commemorate the centenary of the
founding of their original Penny Bazaar here in Kirgate market in

1884. The market also happens to be the largest in Europe on a single site.

The lads wiped their hands and mouths free of grease on the paper serviettes supplied with their burgers and duly placed them in a nearby litter bin. After a quick recce, they joined the rest of the tribe examining a bic-a-brac stall filled with an assortment of trinkets, curios and ornaments.

'Get yer 'ands in yer pockets an' buy summat, yer set o' skinflints!' skitted Roy sarcastically. 'On second thoughts, divent bother,' he uttered, none too quietly after a quick look at the stall's contents. 'It's a load of tat.'

'Aye, yer not wrong,' agreed Ronnie.

'Whey, ar wouldn't say that bonny lads,' said Unlucky Alf who then went on to purchase a cream coloured chalk-like ornament of a Dickensian looking character in a top hat and tails. It was drunken looking, and leaning on a barrel of beer with the words 'Work is the curse of the drinking class' inscribed on the plinth base.

'Very apt that Alfred,' commented John.

'Aye, work certainly never got in the way of his boozing - ditto his mates an' all,' skitted Roy.

Alf just smiled, happy with his purchase, which was all that mattered.

'Ha way then, let's get ganning if yer all done,' said Joseph.

As a group they entered the indoor market. Weaving round the shoppers, they looked around inquisitively with natural interest. Inevitably, Roy's mouth was soon back in gear. 'Ar tell yer what, these Yorkshire bairns aren't slow in coming forwards. When I was waiting for me burger ar heard this sprog talking to his favver. He said, "Daddy, where do babies come from?" After a slight pause his favver says, "The stork brings 'em." Then the kid says, "But who fucks the stork?" Best part though was when his favver says, "I don't know son." Thick Yorkshire man or what?'

Roy got a good laugh in response but it was short lived as Stuart rained on his parade. 'You're a lying git,' he derided.'

'I'm not. Honest.' claimed the disingenuous jester before turning

81

on Stuart. 'You can't 'ave been listening, lost in that little world of yours. Yer big greedy eyes were popping out of their sockets. Yer were mesmerised by them sizzling burgers. I saw yer dribbling down yer chin.'

'Whatever,' was Stuart's droll reply, purposely using the Americanisms he knew Roy detested. All that was loud and vulgar in the Big Apple, in Roy's opinion, invariably crossed the pond and inflicted our fair isle. 'Don't even go there,' went on Stuart. 'Twenty-four seven.'

'Now that is lazy slang,' intervened Fred. 'To say twenty-four hours a day, seven days a week wouldn't kill them.'

'Whey, most of 'em are big fat lard arses anyway. They need to save their breath fer ordering all that junk food,' said Roy scathingly. 'Big Macs wi' giant fries. A Bucket of Haagen-Dazs, then a gallon o' coke to wash it all down. That, or gargantuan pizzas, delivered to the door o' course so they divent exert their sens picking it up. Then the fat bastards 'ave the cheek to turn round an' sue the fast food companies fer mekking 'em overweight. Only in America, eh? You wait - McDonald's an' Co'll move ower to Iraq an' set up shop there soon. Probably 'ave already. McDonald's sprouting up all ower the desert. Ar did read somewhere, they had a plan fer a thousand 50ft inflatable Ronald McDonalds to be scattered around Iraq, but the pilot scheme was shelved after one was downed by a hostile rocket propelled grenade. One of the very few successes for the Iraqi elite republican guard.'

A stoical sigh passed throughout the group but failed to silence Roy who continued with his bullshit.

'Mind you . . . they winna have it all their own way. It's a little known fact, there's a lot o' competition between fast food outlets already in operation. *Burka* King are well established ower there. They winna be happy wi' McDonald's muscling in on their monopoly. Mind . . . 'aving said that, McDonald's 'ave a ready market for their products. There's the hundreds of thousands of troops that invaded - Whoops! I mean liberated Iraq, fer starters. Then there'll be the USA only construction companies on their way to re-build all that infrastructure flattened by their country in the first place. Every cloud 'as a silver lining . . . KFC are starting up a sister branch as well - Kabul Fried Camel. They employ loads of security guards yer nar. You wouldn't believe the fighting that gans on fer who gets the drumstick.'

'You're bloody mental you,' said Billy supressing a smile. 'What gans on in your heed ar divent nar.'

'Just call me 'the enigma' canny lad. That'll dee me.'

The busy Leeds market oozed the cheery weekend atmosphere. That Saturday feeling was alive and kicking. The Monday to Friday workers could relax and paint the town red come nightfall. Getting inebriated as they liked mattered not. Tomorrow was Sunday and the majority of them could lie in with no cursed alarm clock to disturb thir slumber - apart from the hapless few who had forgotten to switch it off.

Markets, shops and department stores throughout the land loved and benefited from the Saturday feel-good factor. Happy shoppers willingly parted with their hard earned money and rightly so - God didn't invent credit cards to be laid dormant in pockets, purses and wallets. Let the devil take tomorrow, for today I have a plastic friend.

The row of butcher's shops was bustling with their brisk Saturday trade. Happy customers departing with one or more blue striped carrier bags, bursting with various meats at prices that wouldn't break the bank. The windows displayed cleverly arranged cuts of meat, enhanced and made even more attractive with well placed lighting that would not look out of place on Leeds City Varieties stage. The whole presentation was enough to entice even the hardened vegetarians.

The butchery business had picked up of late after years of uncertainty brought about through BSE and the foot and mouth outbreak. Thankfully, confidence had gradually returned but there were some who had abandoned meat forever, not convinced of government assurances that meat was now safe to eat.

Stopping off at a seafood stall, the lads bought a tub of prawns each.

'Smells a bit fishy,' said Roy, turning up his nose.

'Whey, what d'yer expect it to smell like? It's a fish food stall - dur - Yer dickhead!' mocked Stuart.

'Aye, yer should be used to it Roy. Same smell as them mingers you pick up now an' again when they're rat-arsed,' ridiculed Billy.

'There's nowt wrong wi' a fishy pair o' slappers knickers, yer ginger twat. Ar love whipping a pair off an' 'aving a reet good sniff. Yer canna whack it man,' said Roy. Popping a prawn in his mouth he turned to the rest of the party, 'Not partaking of the crustacean family gentlemen?' he inquired.

They all declined, preferring to save their appetites for the imminent pub meal.

'Ar divent trust that seafood shite.'

'Elegantly put, Tom lad.'

'Whey, he's reet Ronnie. Yer never nar how fresh it is. Yer could easily end up wi' food poisoning. I did years back after eating some dodgy shrimps in Whitley Bay. An' it wasn't very pleasant, let me tell you. An' look at them slimy oysters there! They're bloody awful! Ar tried one o' them years ago. It was like licking phlegm off a tortoise shell - Urgh!'

'Give it a rest Dennis man,' complained Don. 'Yer putting me off me lunch man!'

'Who are you trying to kid!' skitted Dennis. 'The little bald Sunderland gannet put off 'is grub that easily? Pull the other one, it's got bells on.'

'Hey up!' announced Roy. 'The Three Stooges are warming up. It'll be pistols at ten paces by tea-time, you watch.'

'Just keep that out,' admonished Dennis, touching his nose. 'Forget that Three Stooges crap - The Three Muskateers more like sonny. All for one and one for all.'

'Here here!' cheered Don and Arthur in unison.

'Hey up, visions of grandeur again,' scoffed Roy.

'He's reet, we never argue,' stressed Arthur. 'We're far too civilised fer that. We have, what you call . . . informed debates. Admitted, they might get a little heated on the odd occasion, but we do live in a democracy - Just. Ar've never telt yer this afore, but when Dennis an' I toured the north east clubs, we sort of connected for life. Ar think the equivalent of todays parlance would be . . . we've bonded.'

'Now ar nar fer sure where Roy inherited his codswallop from!' chuckled John.

Roy was baited and couldn't resist a bite. 'You an' Dennis toured the clubs?' he mocked. 'What for? Did they 'ave mobile khazi cleaners in the olden days? Ladies and gentlemen, topping the bill today . . . all the way from Stanhope Weardale . . . Please give a big warm welcome by putting your hands together, for the magnificent . . . Latrine Brothers!'

'We were a very popular singing duo. Yer great pillock. Knickers thrown at us . . . Our dressing rooms under siege . . . It was like Beatlemania. We were massive,' boasted Dennis. 'Went all the way, Arthur and I. We even sang in Washington.'

'That sounds very impressive Dennis, but you conveniently forgot to mention it was Washington Tyne an' Wear!'

'Humph! A mere trifling detail young en.'

'Yes, a slight oversight on my partner's behalf. It's easily done,' voiced Arthur. 'We once sang with Elton John.'

'Of course you did granda,' humoured Roy. 'Did you ever get to sing with the King then?'

'Eeh . . . what are you like? Divent be so daft our Roy. We were only bairns when King George was on the throne.'

'Very witty! Yer nar ar meant Elvis Presley.'

'Oh! The Burger King! Now I'm with you. Why didn't yer say so in the first place, yer daft beggar.' Arthur paused, screwing his forehead as if in deep thought. 'Now let me think . . . Nar, I divent recall singing with Elvis . . . Do you Dennis?

'Nope. Canna say ar do Arthur.'

'Gan on then,' sighed Roy. 'Ar'll be the fall guy. Where was it yer performed with Elton John then? The Albert Hall? Wembley Arena? Stanhope Club? Ha way man, the suspense is killing me,' he mockingly yawned.

Arthur duly obliged his grandson. 'It was in The Dog an' Duck on the karaoke machine - Spennymoor. Candle in the Wind. We brought the house down.'

'What? You were a pair o' terrorists as well?'

'Now yer being stupid.'

'Whey, you started it.'

'Mind you . . . We did go down a bomb - Boom! Boom!'

'Did this worldwide duo have a name then?'

'Wye aye man.'

'That's a queer name.'

'Button it gob-shite! If yer must know, we were called the Symbolics. I was Sym, Dennis was Bolics! Eeh . . . the old ones are the best!'

'I beg to differ. One thing's fer sure, if either of youse could o' ever held a musical note, yer both brilliant at disguising it on the old karaoke machine.'

'Arraway an' shite man. There must be summat wrong wi' your hearing laddie,' pointed out Dennis.

'There's nowt up wi' my lugs ar'll 'ave yer nar. I possess perfect listening organs, thank you very much,' insisted Roy.

They continued on their way through the market.

'Yer see all these pyramids o' beauitiful looking fruit an' what 'ave yers?' observed Frank.

'Aye, what aboot them like?' asked Joseph .

'Whey, it's all fer show man. It's all a front. Tek them apples ower there,' he indicated, pointing to an impressive display of neatly stacked, beautifully polished red apples. 'They're not fer the likes of us my friend. You ask fer a pund o' them an' they'll get 'em from behind the stall, putting 'em in a brown bag afore yer can see 'em. When yer get 'em home yer'll find yer've got a bag of half rotten fruit with a bit o' the decent stuff. Underweight to boot.'

'Ar'll agree with yer there Frank. They keep all the good stuff fer their regulars. Having said that, there are some decent vendors aboot besides the sharks. Them with any commom sense let yer pick yer own. When all's said an' done, palming folks off with iffy goods is like shooting their own fox, so to speak.'

'How'd yer mek that out Joseph?'

'Because bonny lad, anyone with an ounce o' common sense is not ganna go back an' buy their manky products again are they?'

'Aye, ar suppose not,' concurred Frank.

'Me an' our lass do ower shopping at Safeways in Consett but we divent buy their fruit an' veg. It costs an arm an' a leg man. Nar, we nip ower to the nearby outdoor market. The bloke who owns it gives us top quality stuff every time an' it's half the price o' Safeways.'

'Ar canna be arsed wi' all that shopping lark. I leave it to our lass. Stuff that fer a game o' monkeys. If it wasn't for her, ar'd likely starve to death. Nar, ar definitely divent like shops an' the like. I'm uncomfortable now wi' all these crowds. Ar canna wait to get out. I feel boxed in an' I'd of been a lot worse if I hadn't necked a few pints o' dutch courage aforehand.'

'Fear not Franklin, your wish will be shortly granted. The way out's just up ahead,' Joseph reassured him.

Once outside the Vicar Lane exit, Frank gulped in the fresh air. 'Phew, that's better!'

'Aye, it were a bit claustrophobic in there like,' said Tom, who was also enjoying a feeling of break-out. 'It's a canny market mind,' he added before he too took several deep swallows of fresh air - if you could call it fresh air in a major polluted city.

Tom lit up a cigarette to add to the city atmosphere's impurities. Several of his companions followed suit. He spotted a vacant space on a bench. Seats were at a premium, more so on a Saturday than through the week. Squeezing in his bony buttocks with a sigh of comfort, he bid good day to the elderly lady beside him. He was relieved that the rest of the party were taking a fag break, being too proud to ask them to wait-up while he rested.

Roy, mischievous as ever offered to nip back to the bus for old Tom's iron lung to which Tom gave him a sharp rebuff, suggesting he may need to return for a stretcher if he didn't watch his insolence.

After looking every which way, the lads tongues were all but hanging from their mouths. Like kids in a sweet shop, not knowing which way to turn for the plethora of Yorkshire totty. Never had they seen so many young ladies in one place at the same time.

'Down boy,' said Roy, indicating his crotch area.

'Divent fret man, nee one'll notice even if your puny little pecker reaches it's maximum potential of one an' a half inches,' derided Stuart.

'Piss off, yer jealous git. Divent think it's gone unnoticed that more than the odd chick has been scanning my well endowed manhood.'

'Yeah, but that's been the blokes. It's teeming wi' puffs man.'

'Bollocks! Anyway, how can you tell if a blokes's gay or not? Are yer some kind of telephonist or what?'

'You mean am I telepathic, yer big divvy.'

'Yeah, yeah, whatever. Speak to the hand cos the ears ain't listening.'

'It's got nowt to do wi' telepathy, spotting homosexuals. It's more the subtle clues like two blokes walking hand in hand or a couple of 'em kissing an' groping each others arses. Hard to recognise for your average layman - granted.'

'Ar . . . yer clever git. Mind, ar might 'ave guessed you were an expert on gayism behaviour - the big puff that you are.'

'Very original Royston. Been studying again 'ave we?'

'Stop yer bickering,' said Billy. 'Give it a rest, we're on holiday. Relax an' enjoy the view. A few hours from now, we'll be too pissed to tell a fit bird from a dog.'

'Roy has that trouble even when he's sober. Not that that's very often. The word sobriety isn't in his vocabulary,' mocked Stuart.

'Too right it isn't,' was Roy's response, surprisingly without malice.

'I must agree though, the female of the species does look more appealing after a skinful,' added Stuart.

'Bah! Look at that big un! Ar bet she's flattened some grass in her time. Remember that two ton minger I picked up in Whitley Bay a couple o' years back? Ar took her in the sand dunes to slip her a length. Talk aboot fat . . . Ar fumbled aboot amongst her flab fer twenty minutes. In the end I asked her to fart to give us a clue. She didn't take it very well . . . '

'Now there's a surprise,' tutted Stuart.

'Eyes left you two knob jockeys,' announced Roy. 'There's a couple o' corkers heading our way. Play it cool lads. Leave the chatting up to the stud.'

As the two young ladies neared, Roy leered at them giving them the once over. 'Bonjoir bonny lasses. Voulez-vous un soiree avec moi, pet?'

They giggled and carried on. 'What did he say?' one girl asked the other.

'I haven't the foggiest but it's the first French Geordie I've ever come across.'

'Weardaler if yer divent mind!' shouted Roy after them, before adding, 'An' you've left yer tits at home, love! Yorkshire mingers,' he muttered.

'Steady on Roy man,' advised Stuart. 'Yer can be done fer sexual harassment at the drop of a hat these days.'

'Stop fretting man. It's only a bit o' fun.'

'Ar didn't nar you could speak French,' commented Billy.

'Oh, yes son. I'm bi-sexual,' replied Roy.

'I think yer mean bilingual,' chuckled Billy.

'Nar, he was reet in the first place,' Stuart affirmed.

'Shut it, lard heed,' snapped Roy, his eyes still darting everywhere in search of talent. 'A couple of dykes crossing the road ower there,' he indicated. Even ye two imbeciles should be able to pick these out, they stand out a mile. Doc Marten's on their plates o' meat. The one with the short back an' sides with the shirt an' tie'll be the man. She'll 'ave a dildo in transit.'

'How d'yer nar they've got a van?'

'Stewpot, divent be a prick all yer life. Tek a day off.'

'Stuff the lesbos - metaphorically speaking,' said Billy. 'I'm too busy ogling the straight chicks. Well, ar think that's what I'm eyeing. Yer can never be sure these days can yer? Yer could easily end up wi' a ladyboy. Chat her up at a bar . . . After a few sherberts, nip down the nearest alley, tit her up a bit, stick yer hand down the old panties, only to discover a pair o' hairy bollocks an' a throbbing dick!'

'Billy, stop fantasizing again.'

'You must be joking! It's summat ar read aboot, that's all,' stated Billy in his own defence.

'Ar'll believe you, thousands wouldn't,' said Roy sarcastically, before spotting his next prey. 'There's a lass there wi' a ring through her nose,' he pointed out. 'I'm not ower keen on all that body-piercing regalia. They ower do it man. Ar bet you a tenner she's got a ring through her bellybutton an' a stud in her tongue. A bit dodgy that yer nar . . . It could rip yer bell end to shreds. I always mek 'em tek it out afore ganning down fer a blow job.'

'Do you always 'ave to be so graphic?' groaned Stuart. 'You're worse than Chubby Brown!'

'Stop being such a prude Milky. Who are you? Mr Morality or summat? Listen an' learn boyo. Ar once went down . . . '

'Ar wish you would gan down - Six foot under,' muttered Stuart.

'When you've quite finished . . . as I was saying . . . Ar once went down on this slapper an' she had a ring in one of her piss flaps. It must 'ave been a cheap ring cos the next morning me tongue was all green. I assume the cheapskate tart had won it at Stanhope Fair . . . Bah, she could rabbit on - even with her mouth full. Ar telt her not to talk whilst she was performing on the monster. I was scared she'd get tongue-tied.'

Billy and Stuart both shook their heads in resignation.

'You're so full of crap, it's not true,' said Stuart. 'Billy, do you remember last year - that old trout he went out with? He thought he was the world's best shagger, when it turned out she had asthma.'

'Go stuff yer sen, pencil knob. At least ar divent 'ave to resort to giving an empty milk bottle one. So, up yours pal.'

'When you're quite ready gentlemen, we will proceed to the entrance of the nearby Victoria Quarter en route to the pub,' announced Joseph, authoritatively.

'Ha way Tom lad,' said Ronnie, offering his friend a helping hand. 'Time to move on. Our tour guide awaits us.'

Getting up from the bench, Tom let rip a rather loud involuntary fart. 'Eeh . . . hark at me,' he chuckled, not in the least embarrassed. 'Thank God it wasn't a wet one Ronnie lad.'

'Whey, ar suppose that is a blessing Thomas,' laughed Ronnie. 'Yer wouldn't want to be walking aboot in shite encrusted underpants fer the rest of the day.'

'Divent worry bonny lad, I always carry a spare pair o' Y fronts on these trips in case of emergencies.'

'Yer an incorrigible old rogue, but better to be safe than sorry.'

'Aye, well, I was in the scouts yer nar. 'Be prepared' was their motto. An' it's stood me in good stead ower the years.'

The Weardalers were gathered at the pelican crossing. When the green man finally put in an appearance, they set off with the other pedestrian masses. Not even reaching halfway across the road, the green man began frantically flashing to the accompaniment of an annoying high pitched tone, urging everyone to get a move on.

'Stuff 'em. Let 'em wait. I'm not rushing fer anyone,' grumbled Unlucky Alf, his sentiments silently approved by the majority. 'Yer wait patiently by the roadside fer ages an' when you finally get the go ahead yer've got aboot three seconds to get ower t'other side. Linford Christie'd 'ave all on to mek it. Ruddy motorists sat revving their engines as if they're in pole position at Brands Hatch . . . Steam coming off their heeds an' spewing out filthy exhaust fumes. Where's the bloody fire, fer God's sake? A glimpse o' the lights ganning green an' they're off like a bat out o' hell, only to pull up at the next set o' lights fifty yards ahead, if they divent jump a red light that is. A trail o' dead pigeons scattered in their wake. Bloody lunatics man. It's nee wonder there's so much carnage on the roads. Pissed up, drugged up an' just plain idiot dick heads, not fit to drive a dodgem car. Crazy, plain crazy.'

'Mebbe a slight embelishment on your behalf, but ar nar where yer coming from. Well said Alfred,' humoured Joseph.

As if to prove Alf's ramifications, a driver blasted his car horn impatiently. Cool as you like, Alfred, carrying on his way and looking straight ahead, without turning gave the driver the V sign. He padded on to the pavement to the hoots of laughter from his companions, a silent smile on his face.

'Ar hope this boozer's nearby. Ar's spitting feathers man,' said Fred, the rest of the group agreeing with him.

'Okay, ar've got the message. Only another five minutes,' Joseph assured them.

'I'm ready fer a pint or ten meself,' said John. 'This is great, having no responsibilities fer the day,' he said, excitedly rubbing his hands together. 'An' am I ganna mek the best of it or what?'

To be fair to him, when the popular landlord was on one of these outings, he left his business head back home. Where some folks had trouble switching off, not so John. All work and no play? You could stick that for a lark as far as he was concerned. A generous man, he willingly dipped into his pockets on these outings. Buying numerous rounds and even paying for meals on behalf of his regulars. He looked on it as an unofficial 'thankyou' for their year round loyalty. His generosity was much appreciated by his customers, who indeed, were his close friends really, though you'd never hear it from their lips. Besides, words of gratitude were not necessary. He was aware of their appreciation and that's all that mattered to him.

'This is what you call busy, busy. So busy, I said it twice,' stated Billy. 'Give me Stanhope Front Street any day.

'Stop complaining yer big jessie, it's ace! Ar've brushed up against a couple of splendid tits in these crowds,' announced Roy.

'Yer shouldn't talk aboot Alf an' old Tom like that,' quipped Stuart.

Roy ignored his joke. 'Ar've all on stopping me sen from 'aving a grope beneath one o' these micro-skirts the Yorkshire lasses are nearly wearing. Very tempting . . . ' slavered Roy.

'You need to get out more pal.'

'Yer not kidding Stewpot. If ar moved to Leeds, ar'd be walking around wi' a permanent hard on.'

'Divent be getting carried away whatever yer do Roy man. Yer'll be getting us all arrested. If yer touch up a bird these days, yer'll find yer arse in court next day,' said Stuart, only half jokingly.

'What d'yer tek me for - an idiot? An' that's not an invitation for an unwitty retort, so watch yer step.'

'As if. Ar tell yer what Roy . . . Why divent yer get yer sen a small mirror to stick on yer shoe? Then yer can see what colour panties or G string they're wearing. One or more might be going commando.'

'What d'yer tek me for? Some kind of pervert or summat? It's a canny idea mind . . . Why didn't ar think of that? Ar must be slacking.'

'He doesn't need to buy a mirror, he carries one round with 'im all the time. That, an' half a dozen combs,' skitted Billy. 'Thinks he's the Fonz.'

'Er . . . ar think you're getting me mixed up with Stuart the Brylcreem boy there. An' if ar want your opinion, which is highly unlikely, ar'll ask for it, yer ginger minger. An' anyway, there's nowt wrong wi' being well turned out. It's one of the many assets I possess along with my handsome good looks which is obvious. Then there's my brilliant personality of course an' not least, the old trouser snake, reknowned throughout the north east. Coming to a town near you soon ladies . . . Roy - trouser snake Osborne www.co.uk Oh, that reminds me, ar need some more 'passion' business cards printing. Or, ' . . . lurve' cards as ar like to refer to them,' swaggered Roy.

'Oh, show me a home where the buffalo roam and I'll show you a house full os shit,' sang Stuart, to which Roy paid no heed being thicker skinned than Moby Dick.

'Big Issue! Big Issue! Get your Big Issue!' shouted a street vendor.

'What's he selling? asked Roy. 'Big Tissues? Ar canna mek out these flat cap Yorkie's lingo. They wanna speak proper English what like I dee. Bloody Neanderthals.'

Joseph enlightened him.   'He's shouting Big Issue. It's a weekly magazine sold mainly by unfortunate homeless people. They have to pay upfront for the mags at a designated city office an' then sell them to the public at a set price, keeping the difference. Ar think it's a good thing. They're working fer a living an' it must boost their self esteem. It's a good read as well.'

'Big Issue?' asked the vendor as Joseph stopped.

'Ar'll 'ave one son,' said Joseph, delving into his trouser pocket.

'One twenty please,' said the grateful vendor before handing over a magazine and thanking Joseph. 'Big Issue sir?' he asked Roy.

'No thanks, ar get it delivered,' was Roy's glib reply. 'But look after yer sen,' he added.

'I wish I could, but my lumabago is killing me,' replied the seller in a pathetic voice.'

'I nar exactly what yer mean bonny lad. The weight of my wallet in me back pocket plays havoc wi' me lower back,' said Roy walking on.

'The rotten bastard,' said a shocked Stuart to Billy who raised his eyebrows in agreement. 'Ar'll 'ave one please,' he said. 'An' tek no notice of that ignorant prat. He canna read anyway.'

Handing a copy to Stuart, the Big Issue seller just smiled and wished him a nice day.

'Aren't you buying one Billy? Ha way man, get yer hand in yer pocket,' prompted Stuart.

'Nar, it's alreet, ar'll read yours.'

'You won't. Ar divent believe you! Yer just nodded in agreement a minute ago when ar said what a rotten bastard Roy was for not getting one.'

'No ar didn't! Ar rolled me eyes, that's all man. Ar divent recall signing a contract or engraving it in stone. Ye tek too much fer granted, that's your trouble Milky.'

'Yer a bleeding miser like bollock chops! An' he 'as the cheek to call Yorkshiremen tight! Two peas in a pod you pair.'

'It's not a case of that Stewpot man,' chipped in Roy. 'If ar'd o' bought one from him, he'd only waste the brass on drugs an' strong cider an' lager. I'm being cruel to be kind,' he insisted. 'Call it my contribution to society's unfortunate's - Weaning the geezer off his addictions. You've got to look at the big picture bonny lad. Your short termism solutions, by throwing money at 'em does nee one any good in the long run.' Roy pondered a while, 'Divent yer think it's ironic that homeless people drink Tennants?'

'Yer a heartless pillock,' berated Stuart. 'How do you nar what he spends hs earnings on? It could be on food, clothes, books or rent - who nars?'

'You divent half talk a load o' shite,' scoffed Roy. 'How can the geezer be spending money on rent? He's homeless, yer daft get! A cardboard box from the back o' Morrison's winna cost him owt. He saw ye coming Milky boy. Yer a soft touch!'

'Remind me to put you forward for humanitarian of the year award Osborne. Or mebbe the Nobel peace prize.'

'Aye, ye do that muggins. An' there'll be plenty more bleeding hearts lining up to relieve yer of yer wodge this afternoon an' all. It's true what they say - There's one born every minute. Yer'll see dolly birds floggin' enamel badges "For the baby incubator's association sir" or whatever. If you're lucky, five pence in the pund ending up to the charity, an' the rest of the brass split between the dolly birds an' the organisers - con men - that is. They winna divulge that info your way though. Oh, it'll be there alright, buried in the small print fer legality reasons. But yer'll need Patrick Moore's telescope to read it.'

'You're street savvy fer somebody who hardly ever leaves Stanhope,' remarked Stuart.

'What can ar say? I'm well read. I 'ave to be. Ar need to keep on top of me general knowledge, plus all the topical issues, so as ar can debate, nar . . . argue with my know-it-all cousin, Alistair.' Roy glanced at his watch, 'Ten past one. Einstein should be supping 'is first half pint round aboot now. He'll 'ave just finished 'is part-time job as bouncer at Mothercare half an hour ago. One o'clock on the dot, Mr Punctuality'll 'ave walked into Whitelocks. He's never late. We're ganna have to get some ale down him - see if we can mek 'im less boring. Ar doubt it though. Do yer nar . . . the last time he got pissed was when Myra Hindley finally kicked the bucket. Mind yer, we all pushed the boat out that day. We were rat-arsed, if yer ken.'

'Aye, too bloody reet we did.' Stuart agreed wholeheartedly. 'They should've hanged that child torturing murdering bitch years ago along with that Ian Brady. An eye fer an eye it sez in the bible.'

'Divent start quoting the bible. Ar divent agree they should've hanged Brady an' Hindley.'

'What? Did ar hear reet?' gasped Stuart. 'Is this the new softer, more tolerant side of Royston Osborne, never, ever seen before? Quick, get me a brandy. I'm in a state of shock!'

'If you'd shut up an' let me finish, motor-mouth, yer'd nar the reason. They shouldn't 'ave hanged, because hanging's too good for 'em. They should 'ave been handed over to the parents an' families o' them poor bairns. Locked in a room with 'em to dish out some proper justice.'

95

'That's more like the Roy ar nar. You 'ad me worried there fer a minute.'

'No need to fret on that score man. Ar'll not turn into some shite liberal, tree hugging 'All you need is love' dickhead. Just tek a look at this country . . . the crime capitol of Europe. These soft-as-shite do-gooders 'ave a lot to answer for - the tossers.'

'Don't hold back Roy. You say what yer mean.'

'Orh . . . Bollocks to the lot of 'em! Life's too short.'

Billy caught up to Roy and whispered in his ear. Roy nodded his head and Billy dropped back to the rear of the group. A few seconds later Roy's mobile phone rang to the familiar strains of 'You're so vain.' Removing it from his pocket he answered, 'Hello, the stud at your service.'

Stuart felt something was afoot, having been left out of the short discussion between his two mates, he was feeling somewhat miffed.

Roy spoke in a loud voice so as the rest of the Stanhope Massive could hear. 'Oh dear . . . Really? Whey, that's not on is it? Turned up out of the blue you say? Yeah. Yeah. I'm sorry to hear that Gladys. Try not to worry pet. Aye, will do. Bye fer now Gladys.' Switching off his mobile, he returned it to his pocket, winking at Stuart as he did inviting him to move closer to the group.

Billy had meanwhile pocketed his mobile and rejoined the rest of the party.

John, who didn't own a mobile by choice, despite Gladys's protestations, had heard the conversation and Roy was now calling out his name.

'What can I do for you laddie?'

'Whey, fer starters, yer'd better brace yer sen fer some bad news,' announced Roy.

'Gan on then, I'm all ears.'

'Your lass has just phoned me from out of the blue.'

'Ar've told her not to drink in that dive!' joked John. 'Why didn't yer pass her on to me?' he asked, not really sure whether this was a wind up or not.

'Because she was in such a rush and sounded very agitated.'

'What did she want then?'

'They've shut down The Phoenix until futher notice.'

'Who have?'

'The customs an' excise gestapo. They've paid your premises an unexpected visit and forced Gladys to cease trading forthwith.'

John's head was now racing. His immediate thought was some local busybody had shopped him for running an illegal bookmakers from his pub.

'Yer joking aren't you? Tell me it's a wind up,' he said rapidly, not knowing what to think. 'Did our lass mention betting? I'm dead if she did,' he fretted.

'Nar, nowt like that man. Calm down,' said Roy, now thoroughly enjoying himself. 'They just came to check yer beers an' spirits.'

'Phew! Thank God fer that!' John's relief was palpable. 'I'm alright then. They'll be checking I'm serving the right measures. Aye, that's it.'

'You're in the shit then,' skitted Frank.

'Shut it, I'm trying to think here . . . Wait on a minute . . . ' he paused, carefully gathering his thoughts together. 'They wouldn't shut down the pub fer a few measures. Are you telling me lies, bollock chops? Because if you are, ar'll ruddy well kill you.'

'Hey, steady on man. Divent shoot the messenger! All I nar, via your good lady, is that one of these customs an' excise geezers pulled a pint of yer ale an' traces of alcohol were found in it.'

'You little shit! Ar should 'ave known you were pulling me chain! I don't believe it!'

John made to go for Roy who was already making a hasty retreat anyway, laughing his head off, safe in the knowledge John would soon see the funny side. John's revenge would come later, when Roy least expected it.

Chapter 6

'Here we are then, The Victoria Quarter,' announced Joseph. 'This is where the more affluent shop. Or, put it another way - people with more money than sense. It's that posh, the shop assistants fart into a handkerchief.'

'Eeh . . . you are a wag,' said Dennis, with a touch of sarcasm.

Joseph took no heed and carried on with his enlightening commentary. 'For those of you who are interested, keep glancing up above. The structure is very impressive.'

'Tosser,' muttered Roy.

'Not a culture lover then, ar tek it?' said Stuart.

'Culture? Show me some an' ar'll let yer nar.'

The arched glass roof of both arcades featured leaded lights and stretched from Vicar Lane to Briggate. They were both linked by a central corridor and made up the prestigious Victoria Quarter which had been elaborately refurbished some years earlier. The lower arcade boasted an impressive central fountain. This would be turned off in the run up to Christmas to accommodate a tall, cone shaped Christmas tree, adorned with exquisite decorations. The curved green balcony railings above the shops ran the full length of the complex and the glass facades of the shops had been carefully preserved to lose none of their original charm.

'There's nee prices on these clothes,' pointed out Alf, looking in a shop window displaying only one outfit of clothes on one faceless mannequin.

'That's because if yer need to nar the price, yer probably canna afford them,' Joseph enlightened him. 'Yer not in Netto land here old boy. It's all expensive designer clothing. How can I put it?' he mused, 'Let's just say, these opulent shops cater for the more discerning shoppers.'

'What's that mean in English?'

'For rich bastards basically Alfred. An' there's more than a few o' them in Leeds, ar can tell yer. They canna build half a million to a million pund luxury apartments quick enough.'

'Folks must 'ave more money than sense, that's all ar can say.'

'I have to disagree with yer there Fred. If people 'ave the brass to buy an apartment - why not? When yer think aboot it, it meks sense. Saves all the hassle of getting in an' out of the centre o' Leeds if yer work there.'

'Aye, ar suppose yer reet Joseph, put like that.'

'Hey up chaps, there's a massage parlour here!' beckoned Roy.

'Pedicures, skincare, massage,' read Billy. 'Ar divent think it's the kind of massage parlour you're thinking aboot Roy.'

'How do ye nar? Nip in an' see will yer?'

'Like hell ar will,' objected Billy.

'Aye yer reet, they're more likely to give a proper massage to somebody rugged, with looks to die for . . . Me fer instance.'

'Gan on then Roy,' dared Billy.

'Whey, ar would, but ar divent want to be late meeting ower Alistair. It wouldn't be fair,' bluffed Roy. 'Mebbe another time.'

'An' pigs might fly.'

Arthur was looking in a ladies clothes shop.

'Yer not a closet transsexual are yer Arthur?' teased Don.

Arthur ignored Don's remark and addressed the group, 'Ar bet a hundred pund, none of youse lot nar what this shop used to be,' he challenged.

'What are we supposed to be, psychic or summat? I d'nar. A pub,' guessed Dennis.

'Nope.'

'A cinema?' suggested Frank.

'Nope.'

'It could've been anything. What decade are we talking aboot, the 80s?' asked Joseph.

'Nar, it wasn't when you were living in Leeds Joseph. Tell yer what, ar'll give yer a clue cos it's a hard one. I'm talking, the early 60s.'

'That's before ower time,' chuntered Stuart.

'True. You young ens aren't in on this.'

'An Italian cafe,' speculated old Tom.

'Nope. Yer'll never guess it, so ar'll put yer out of yer misery. It was a Mecca dance hall,' announced Arthur with smug satisfaction. 'I came in here in 1962 or 63. Jimmy Saville was the DJ. Not long after that he opened his own club, The Three Coins, I think it was, here in Leeds. The rest is history - as they say.'

'Whey, yer learn summat every day,' remarked Dennis.

'Aye, well remembered Arthur,' said Frank.

'I divent nar how I remembered the name of the club,' said Arthur. 'Ar haven't thought aboot it for years. Eeh, happy memories,' he reflected as they walked on.

'That was interesting,' yawned Roy. 'Ar nearly nodded off there,' he muttered to the lads.

'I didn't find it boring. I find things like that really interesting,' said Stuart.

'You wanna get out more bonny lad.'

The Weardalers had a quick look in a Vivian Westwood shop before stopping at the shop directly opposite. On display were Steiff bears, Rag Dolls, ornamental figures and quality knick-knacks.

'Ar see there's nee prices again,' pointed out Fred.

'That's because it'd put yer off ganning inside the shop. It's like ar said earlier,' Joseph reminded them, 'Folks who shop in these places divent need to worry aboot prices.'

'Eeh look, there's a golliwog! Ar've not seen one o' them in a long while,' proclaimed Alf.

'Shush man. That could be construed as racism,' pointed out Roy.

'Give ower.'

'He's reet Alf,' confirmed Stuart. 'Yer canna say golliwog anymore. Yer've got to call 'em Golly persons or just plain golly.'

'Yer pulling me leg!'

'He's telling the truth Alf,' Don assured him.

101

'Whey, this country's gone mad, that's all ar can say!'

'Aye, tell us summat we divent nar,' sighed John. 'The lunatics 'ave tekken over the asylums alreet. An' the asylum seekers as well come to that.'

'Hey look, there's a group of dwarfs heading our way,' pointed out Roy. 'There must be a circus in town. Ar bet they can't be called dwarfs anymore either with all this PC shite.'

'Correct bonny lad. They're now called vertically challenged people,' said Don. 'Or P.O.R.G - Persons of restricted growth. Ar wouldn't mind, but the majority of them couldn't care less aboot being called dwarfs. They just get on with it. I saw a programme about them a few months back. They run successful companies an' all sorts. Very determined individuals they are. Some conventional sized folks could learn a thing or two from them.'

'Ar bet slappers love them,' smirked Roy. 'They'll be able to lick the beaver standing up.'

'We can always rely on ye Roy, to drag the coversation into the gutter,' groaned Alf.

'I'm only pointing out one of the advantages of being a dwarf, that's all!'

'Here we are then, the famously renowned Briggate!' Joseph informed them. 'For those who are not in the know, you will notice it has been pedestrianized - much to the delight of Leeds shoppers. Not so long ago, you'd 'ave been lucky to get from one end of Briggate to the other wi'out choking on petrol an' diesel fumes first. It was end to end wi' buses. Ar should nar, ar was one o' the drivers.'

'Hang on a minute, ar'll just nip in Debenhams - see if they've got a soap box,' skitted Fred.

'Very funny Frederic. If yer divent want me to impart a little local information just say so. It meks no odds to me,' carped Joseph, taking umbrage over Fred's remarks.

'Whoo! Steady on lad! Ar was only jesting man. You carry on. I'm sure everyone's genuinely interested in what yer have to say.'

'I'm not,' whispered Billy. 'Ar just want a pint.'

Joseph duly carried on with his address. 'In 1207 Maurice Paynel, the lord of the manor, granted leeds its first borough charter. As well as giving personal freedom to the burgesses of Leeds, it effectively laid the foundations of a 'new town' along the line of a street north of the crossing of the river Aire.' Having recited these facts from memory, Joseph had obviously come prepared as he now delved into his back pocket and pulled out some sheets of written notes.

Roy groaned quietly, 'On no, the boring sod's brought an encyclopaedia.'

'That's a big word for you Roy,' skitted Stuart.

'Ah well, I'm not just a pretty face yer nar.'

'That's your opinion.'

'If ar could have your undivided attention!' heralded Joseph, shooting a withering look in the direction of the lads, 'I'll carry on. This street was wide enough to accommodate a market, and on either side were thirty burgage plots of building land, which have since been pinpointed with the old inn yards - well worth a look while you're here - which are shown on 19th century maps. The street became lined with shops and houses with open courts, gardens and tenter grounds. For those of you not familiar with the word 'tenter' - it's a frame on which cloth is stretched out to dry without losing its shape.'

'Eeh, who'd of thought? Ar'll sleep better tonight knowing that,' whispered Roy.

'There was no bridge over the river Aire at the time of the charter. The earliest citation found to a bridge is in the late fourteeenth century, but the street became known as Briggate - the road to the bridge - with the name appearing in documents from the early sixteenth century onwards. Right gentlemen, any questions?'

'Aye, thanks fer that info Joseph. Can yer tell me where Borders bookstore is sited?' asked Arthur.

'Just up the street a bit on this side, right next to McDonalds, which was, I might add, up until recently 'Wendy Burger' - another American fast food outlet,' Joseph reliably informed him.

'Cheers, ar'll nip in later with our Alistair an' 'ave a look round.'

'Ar tell yer what, there's every nationality ganning here,' remarked Stuart looking around. 'We divent even see a darkie back home. It's a great big melting pot here.'

'Most British cities are multi-cultural now, an' 'ave been fer some time,' said John.

'Never mind aboot melting pots, let's get to that pub fer a great big pot of ale. Ar's fair parched,' bemoaned Fred.

'Here here! Let the imbibing commence,' said Alfred grinning, his few remaining yellow teeth showing.

'Ha way then, the pub's just ower the road an' down a bit, in Turk's Head yard. It's that ginnel just afore Marks and Spencer's,' said Joseph leading the way.

'Whey, ar'll gan to ower house, they've got a picture of you there,' said Roy referring to a picture of William Younger, the white bearded old man of the ale advertisements of the same name.

'Ar canna see ye lasting the day Sonny Jim,' warned old Tom, giving Roy a slap on the back of the head.

'Bless you,' said Ronnie after Fred sneezed.

'Thank you kind sir.'

'Do yer nar?' said Don, 'When you sneeze and someone says bless you, it's because it's said to keep out the devil.'

Roy shook his head, 'Ar can see it's ganna be a long day,' he yawned loudly. 'If yer've got anymore snippets of magnificent wisdom, keep 'em to yer sen will yer Kojak?

They turned into Turk's Head yard where Alistair was waiting for them.

'Over here grandad!' he called, his face lighting up on spotting the Weradale clan. He stood up from his seat, a wooden slatted bench sited opposite Whitelock's entrance. A half supped pint of bitter sat before him on a table made from a wooden barrel.

'Hey up Alistair! How yer ganning bonny lad!' greeted Arthur, really pleased to see his grandson and giving him a long hug. 'Not had too many bevvies yet ar hope?'

'It's my first pint grandad. You know me. . . steady as she goes. Everything in moderation.'

'Aye, ar do lad. Unlike our Roy, unfortunately,' sneered Arthur, loud enough for Roy's ears.

'Ar nar yer divent mean that granda, so ar'll let yer off this

104

once,' was Roy's surprisingly genial response. 'How are yer kidder? Not ower deeing it in the brain cell department ar tek it? All work an' no play meks Jack a dull boy, an' all that.'

'Never. The more you keep the old grey matter ticking over, the better,' replied Alistair.

Roy looked round the yard noticing a gutter channel running against the wall behind the benches. 'Old Tom was saying how 'e were surprised yer hadn't arranged to meet up in the Central Library instead of some sixteenth century alleyway smelling o' piss!'

'Ar never said no such thing!' objected Tom. 'Tek nee notice of the mixing little so an' so. We've had to put up wi' this claptrap all morning.'

'It's alright Tom, I believe you. I know what he's like. Some things'll never change, Roy being one of them.'

'Ar bet there's been a canny few robberies an' murders in this alleyway ower the centuries,' commented Fred. 'Eeh . . . ar've got this eerie feeling like I've stepped back in time.'

'Whey, that's because yer have bonny lad,' said Alf. 'Ar tell you what . . . I'd like to be a fly on the wall fer a day sometime in the past. Ar'd love to see what life was like in bygone days.

'Aye, interesting nee doubt,' agreed Tom. 'But when yer think aboot the conditions they had to endure, a fleeting glimpse is all yer'd need. All that poverty an' squalor . . . the workhouses . . incurable diseases. It must 'ave been a nightmare man. Infant mortality rates were horrendous. They didn't 'ave all these modern medicines we tek fer granted. Eeh, it doesn't bear thinking aboot. Let's change the subject. Hey Roy!'

'What?'

'We were just saying like - It's so narrow an' high walled in this alleyway - It'll never get any sun.'

'Your point being?'

'Whey, yer should be alreet fer a few hours yet.'

The old boys chuckled, Tom having inferred that Roy, being the vampire they insinuated he was, would be safe from any sunlight turning him into a plie of dust.

'Very funny Thomas, but please, excuse me, I'm talking to this

105

100 year old gentleman. He says his eyesight isn't quite what it used to be, but he swears he nars you from the past. He thinks it was the early 1920s on Leeds City Varieties stage. Apparently you were sweeping it!' Roy turned back to the lads, 'Reet girls. Ar's ready fer a pint. What we deeing? Supping in rounds or ganning solo? I'm easy either way.'

'Why divent ye young ens sup together,' suggested Arthur. 'The four old boys can argue amongst their sens as usual, an' the rest of us'll drink in rounds. Ar'll get Joseph a pint afore he gans off sightseeing. Right then, we're all sorted - lovely jubbly,' he said Del Boy style, rubbing his hands together.

'Ar never knew yer had a degree in mathematics granda.'

'Are ye being flippant aboot my brilliant drinking strategy laddie?' said Arthur, grabbing Roy in a playful headlock.

'Yer choking me man!' he pleaded.

'Would yer squeeze 'is neck just a little harder while yer at it Arthur?' requested Billy.

'Your wish is my command.' Arthur obliged by feigning to strengthen his hold, but Roy still squealed like a stuck pig.

'Ar canna breathe man! Yer've got me windpipe trapped granda!'

'Arrh . . . yer a big Jessie, nowt else,' scorned Arthur, releasing Roy.

'Ar fooled yer! Ar didn't feel a thing,' said Roy, an inane grin on his face.

'After you.'

'No, after you.'

'No, I insist. You gan ahead.'

Alistair was laughing. 'I see the old boys ritual of getting to the bar last hasn't change then.'

'And it winna. Not until they're six feet under,' sighed Dennis, watching as Fred finally took the initiative and impatiently barged through the pub door first, the rest of old boys in quick pursuit, each of them inwardly smiling to themselves in sheer relief.

'Right. Dennis, Arthur, Frank an' Baldy, what yer all 'aving? Or is that a daft question?'

'Aye it is, but good of you to ask, all the same. Scotch Bitter all round,' said Dennis taking it upon himself to answer on behalf of them all.

'How aboot you Joseph? Is it a pint or are you on the soft drinks?'

'Ar'll 'ave a pint o' Scotch Bitter as well. Thank you very much, mine host.'

'Lads! Is it the same for you?'

'Whey, we were ganna drink in groups John,' pointed out Stuart.

'Never mind all that nonsense fer now. I'm in the chair,' insisted John.

'That's very kind of you landlord,' fawned Roy. 'Three pints of Scotch Bitter an' a shandy fer our Alistair.'

'Is he pulling my plonker or what? Do yer want a pint Alistair?'

'Just a half for now please John.'

'I don't do 'alves son,' pointed out John, doing a quick head count. Nine pints it is then. Give us a hand someone will yer?'

'I'm reet behind you,' obliged Joseph, following in John's wake.

'Salt of the earth our landlord,' muttered Dennis. 'Divent tell him mind - he might stick 'is prices up. Especially when he finds out what they're charging in 'ere. If ar recall, last time I was in 'ere, it were a bit dearer than yer average. A canny pint mind, all the same.'

'He gets all ower the place Dennis man. Cost of a pint winna bother John,' said Arthur.

'Mebbe not, but ar bet you a pund he moans like hell ower the cost when he comes back.'

'Reet, you're on.'

Arthur and Dennis sealed their wager with a handshake.

'The money he meks oot of us, he could afford to pay five pund a pint,' skitted Roy.

'So what? That's what he's in business for man,' maintained Stuart. 'To mek brass. It's not compulsory to gan in the Phoenix all the time. No one's holding a gun to your heed. Ar nar you'd be greatly missed - not . . . But ar think we'd get ower it.'

Roy didn't reply, his attention now elsewhere. 'Ar've been watching this bloke since we came in,' he stated. 'He's never had a cigarette out of his mouth. He smokes more than a beagle.' He was disappointed when his joke fell on deaf ears. Miserable sods he pondered silently.

'How's the security business ganning Alistair?' inquired Arthur. 'Ar should imagine in today's lawless epidemic, your firm'll be thriving.'

'Not enough hours in the day grandad. If I wanted, I could work all the hours God sends, but I try to limit myself to fifty or fifty-five hours a week. I've got to draw the line somewhere, I'd have no time to write my novel.' Alistair sidled up closer to his grandad and whispered to him, 'Plus, I'm presently courting grandad. She's in Leeds today, shopping with her sister.'

'An' 'as this lass got a name?'

'Sorry grandad. She's called Janet. To tell you the truth, I'm a bit worried because she said she might call in here with their Linda for a drink.'

'Whey, that's great news! Ar'll get to meet the lass. But what's the problem son?'

'Do I really need to answer that grandad?'

The penny dropped with Arthur. 'Ah . . . say no more. I've got yer - Our Roy. Yer mustn't tek any heed of yer big-mouthed cousin. It's you that's courting this lass, not him. 'Ave yer not put her in the picture regards Roy?'

'I have, yes. I've warned her about him.'

'Well, there yer are then. Stop fretting.'

'Okay, I will,' smiled Alistair, all the better for his chat to his grandad.

Billy sat down beside Alistair. 'How's tricks kidder? Are yer keeping busy?'

'I can't complain Billy. Overworked and underpaid like most, but that's life,' sighed Alistair.

'Yer not kidding. Me an' Roy are toying wi' the idea o' ganning to work abroad. There's nowt set in concrete yet mind - No pun intended.'

'How is the building game these days? Plenty of work to go at?'

'Not a great deal. We're doing better than most but we seem to be travelling further an' further afield chasing work. Hence ower thoughts on broadening our horizons while we're still young an' unattached. Who nars? Only time will tell.'

'Our Roy's been unattached from reality all his life,' laughed Alistair.

'Yer can say that again.'

'Seriously though Billy, working abroad sounds like a good idea to me - apart from you being saddled with our Roy that is. Won't you miss Stanhope?'

'Yes an' no. Spring an' summer's great back home. Winter's another kettle o' fish. It's ower depressing man. Short days an' long dark nights. Stanhope's like a ghost town. Thank God fer the local pubs an' the club, they help keep yer sane. Ar'll re-phrase that. They keep some of us sane,' chuckled Billy.

'A lot of people suffer in the winter through lack of daylight yer know,' said Alistair. 'The medical term is SAD - Seasonal affective disorder. Some people plug in a bright lamp. It's supposed to lift your mood. Take me now for instance - I can't wait to get back to Stanhope tonight for a fortnight's holiday. But I suppose winter looses its attraction as you grow up. When you're a kid you can always find something to do. You never get bored - at least I didn't.'

'Whey, yer nar, the Eastgate Cement Works shut down last year.'

'I do know. Not good news for local employment.'

'Yer not kidding. Still,' said Billy with resignation in his voice, 'There is nee jobs fer life anymore. 'Asn't been fer a long time when yer think on. According to me favver, apprenticeships were the thing in his day. You left school an' went straight into work learning a skilled trade. When you were twenty one, you were fully trained an' qualified and stayed to work fer the same firm. Nowadays they just use slave labour. These asylum seekers aren't supposed to work, so it's all cash in hand. Yer employers divent have to pay any insurance, sick pay or hoilday money . . . They're loving it. Anyway, back to jobs for life - Personally, ar wouldn't stick in the same job fer life even if ar could. Variety is the spice, as they say - not stagnation. What do you say Alistair?'

'You're right. I totally agree with you Billy. I've no intentions fitting security alarms for the rest of my life. Ideally, I'd like to do something in the literary field for a living. A playwright or a full-time novelist maybe . . . though I'm under no illusions just how hard-earned that would be. Every man and his dog have a book out these days.'

'Isn't it nigh impossible to get a publisher to tek you on?'

'It is that Billy. There's more chance of Roy becoming a monk. I'm going to self-publish. I've read up on it. Life's too short to be sending manuscripts to these London publishing houses. They wouldn't take a chance on a new author anyway, so what's the point? All they're interested in is autobiographies of the already rich and famous - or any old has-been gangster or fraudster or anyone with a sex scandal behind them - which is fair enough, because they're guaranteed to make a tidy profit on these sort of books. They play safe. Who can blame them? People want to read that kind of garbage, so why not supply it? I might start up a publishing company myself one day. They're few an' far between up north, so there's definitely a gap in the market there.'

'Whey, good luck to whatever you decide in the future Alistair. An' ar can drink to that cos here comes John and Joseph wi' the ale.'

'By heck, it's bloody heaving in there! An' the price of the ruddy ale? It's scandalous man!' complained John. 'Ar think Yorkshire's copying London pub prices. Roll on happy hour, that's all ar can say.'

'Huh! You'll be lucky John, they don't have happy hour on a Saturday,' Alistair informed him. 'It's not necessary, there's no shortage of customers on a weekend.'

'What are you complaining aboot anyway John?' interrupted Roy, lighting up another cigarette. 'You never 'ave happy hour on a Saturday either - or on any other day of the week fer that matter.'

'I don't need to. My prices are equitable every day. I've no need for cheap gimmicks,' said John proudly and with justification.

'You're a lot dearer than the club,' stated Roy, undeterred.

'An' ar've telt yer afore, countless times - Go drink down the club then! Give us all some peace.'

Roy ignored John's remark, his mind was working overtime in

110

search of his next wind-up. 'Bah, it's a grand drop of ale this,' he gloated, licking the froth from his lips. 'Ar canna remember when ar had such a fine pint of beer.'

'Pull the other one,' derided John. 'It's the best pint yer've had since yer don't know when, cos it's free.'

'Ar resent those remarks mine host. The fact that it happens to be 'gratis' doesn't enter into the equation. Ar speak as ar find. Roy looked about him, 'Yer pick a strange place fer a rendezvous our Alistair. This 'ere alleyway is like summat straight out of a Jack the Ripper film.'

'I chose this location simply because in my opinion it's the best pub in Leeds,' said Alistair guardedly.

'Whey the beer's certainly up to scratch. Credit where credit's due Yorky.'

'Steady on Roy! You're getting dangerously close to giving me a compliment,' said Alistair in amazement.

'Divent gan owerboard bonny lad.'

'And don't you go overboard wi' that beer,' advised Alistair. 'It's a lot stronger than anything you drink back in Stanhope.'

'Any ale's stronger than John's witch-piss, but divent worry on my account. Ar've supped some potent stuff in my time ar can tell you. Divent tek my word fer it - Judge me at the end of the neet. Look at me an' think of that Elton John song.'

'Which song was that then, Bullshit in the Wind?' mocked Alistair.

'Very droll, Yorky boy, ar don't think. The song I'm referring to is "I'm Still Standing." That lot'll be spark out at the end of the neet - pissed as newts. Whereas my goodself will subsequentially be reet as rain.'

Alistair couldn't help but smile at Roy's deliberate mis-pronunciations. Comical, obnoxious, even a right despicable bastard at times. The studious Alistair could only summon up his loud brash cousin as an enigma.

Arthur handed over a pound coin to Dennis, having lost his small wager with regards to John's complaint about the price of beer.

'Aye aye, what's all this then Arthur?' the transaction not having

111

gone unnoticed by John. "Ave yer started giving brass away?'

'That'll be the day,' skitted Don. 'He's as tight as a duck's arse.

'An' who's rattled your cage? Gan an' polish your heed or summat,' berated Arthur. 'Business discussed between Mr Melly and myself is strictly for ower ears, and, if needs be, my Weardale colleagues only. Ye macam outsiders are welcome amongst us - up to a point. As long as ye divent cross that divide an' accept that ye'll never be ower equals, yer'll be okay. No offence bonny lad. It's just the north east pecking order. Just nar yer station, that's all I'm saying.'

Arthur's face never varied from austere so Don decreed a little counter attack was in order. 'Yer all the same, you inbred hillbillies. Yer've lived in a small minded village fer far too long, that's your problem. Bloody Nazi bigots. Ar could go on, but ar'll keep the conversation civilised on account of it being a day out an' a cordial affair. So, with that ar'll raise my glass an' propose a toast.' Don lifted his glass, 'To the Weardale masons - May your narrow-mindedness live on.'

'Is he tekking the piss or what?' asked Joseph.

'Sounds like it to me,' said Dennis before proposing a counter toast. 'To the slap-heeded Sunderland exile - May he last the day long without being accidentally pushed in front of a bus.'

To the raucous cheers of the Weardalers, Don drank through a wry smile. He pondered briefly on his good fortune in choosing to move from Sunderland to Stanhope. If he hadn't, he'd never have met this rag-tag set of scoundrels - his drinking companions, and though he'd never admit it, much, much more.

'There's a canny few folks sat further up this alley,' remarked John. 'Is there another bar or summat?'

'Yeah it is,' replied Alistair. 'It's another bar belonging to Whitelocks. Between here an' there, you've got the luncheon room and kitchen. As you know, they're reknowned for their roast beef and Yorkshire Pudding.'

'I certainly do young man. My colleagues and I shall shortly be partaking of the aforementioned nourishing fare. Ar can hardly wait, but we shall firstly imbibe of another pint of Whitelock's finest - second only in quality to my fine ales back home.'

'You're absolutely spot on my favourite landlord,' genuflected Dennis. 'Exquisitely put, if I may be so bold sir. Yor modesty humbles me.'

'What's all this hogwash? 'Ave ar missed summat? Has a Tardis transported us back to Dickensian times?' mocked Arthur.

'Shut up man. I'm fishing fer another free pint here, courtesy of mine host,' whispered Dennis.

'Ar heard that Melly! An' yer've nee chance. Try again when I'm comatosed.'

'Whey, that's good enough for me Jonathan. Ar'll hold yer to it mind.'

'Ar've no doubt you will Dennis - divent sweat man. The money ar've made out of ye lot ower the years, ar could afford to buy a round for everyone in Leeds.'

'Ar can believe that an' all,' skitted Dennis. 'One of these days yer might consider treating us all to a proper outing instead o' cheap day trips. How aboot a long weekend away, all expenses paid, just to show your appreciation of our undying loyalty to your alehouse? London . . . Paris maybe . . . better still, Amsterdam! We're not ower fussy are we Arthur?'

'That's reet Dennis. Easy to please - that's us. So long as we stay in a five star hotel . . . we should be adamant aboot that mind.'

'Do yer nar, it's funny you should broach the subject at this time,' said John with slow deliberation. 'Ar was just saying to ower lass recently how you lot merited an excursion of sorts on a larger scale.'

'Now yer talking John boy,' said Dennis, speaking for the rest of them who were all ears. 'And what, may I ask was your good lady's response? Favourable I trust?'

'Would you like the whole nine yards of Gladys's reactions?'

'Aye, carry on.'

'Well, if my memory serves me well, her exact words were - and I quote, "Only when hell freezes over and you become teetotal," the latter being the least likely, obviously. Then she rolled aboot on the lounge carpet laughing that much she wet her sen.'

'Highly amusing I don't think,' said Dennis, a little peeved whilst the rest of the party laughed.

'While ar think on, will yer show me round that Border's Bookstore later on Alistair? Ar want to look up some Leeds United memorabilia.'

'No problem grandad. Just let me know when, an' I'm all yours.'

'Cheers bonny lad. Ar'll buy yer a pint fer yer trouble.'

'There's no need to buy me a pint grandad, it'll be a pleasure. Book shops are my favourite places. Them and libraries.'

'Nevertheless, you're having a pint on me. Subject closed.'

'Fair enough, if you insist. Thanks grandad.'

'Bleeding hell!' exclaimed Roy. 'It's like University Challenge. Ooh look! Here comes Bamber Gasoline.'

'Bamber Gascoigne to be precise,' corrected Alistair. 'But he stopped doing University Challenge years ago. Jeremy Paxman hosts it now. You should start watching. Yer might learn something.'

'Arraway an' shite man. Life's too short to watch a load of pompous egotistic tossers racing to be first to push a buzzer to tell us what a grain of sand weighs. Who gives a shite? Ar divent for one.'

'I have to back Roy up on this one Alistair. No offence like,' said Stuart.

'Pray, go on Stuart, I'm intrigued in what wisdom you have to part.'

'Whey, it's simple really. There's not much point in Roy advancing what little knowledge he has by trying to stimulate his pea brain.'

'Watch it sonny,' warned Roy.

'I'm only being logical here Royston. For you to learn even a smidgen of general knowledge through education, be it television, libraries or even university . . . '

'Hold yer 'orses a minute grease-ball. Now yer really are talking bollocks. Ar'd need to win the lottery to afford university fees, if ar wanted to gan there - which ar don't.'

'Okay, I hear what you're saying Royston, but let's get back to my original point. What I'm saying is you don't have to be Einstein or Steven Hawkins to flip burgers an' serve fries - No brains required, apply within - should suffice in your case.'

'Gan stuff yer sen!' retorted Roy. 'This from a prat that delivers milk fer a living. Able to read 'One extra pinta please' being the only criteria for the job. Divent mek me laugh. An' wi' the rapid decline o' doorstep deliveries, yer'll be lucky to get a job picking fruit an' veg alongside the illegal asylum seekers. Mind you, if yer sign on the dole as well, yer'll be better off. Hold on a sec, that's got me thinking. Ar might be on to summat here . . . Rent free house . . . all yer utility bills paid . . . food . . . Claim fer half a dozen fictitious sprogs . . . They wouldn't check up on yer cos that'd be racism. Yer solicitor'd be quick to point that out - Infringement of human rights . . . This is sounding better all the time. A bit of working on the side, cash in hand, nudge nudge. Is it any wonder the fuckers are clambering to get ower here, crossing the channel clinging to blown-up rubber johnnies. Mind you, it's nice to see ower taxes going to worthwhile causes. Billy!'

'Yeah, what can ar do for yer?'

'Ar've come up with a great idea.'

'Oh aye, an' what's that then?'

'Firstly, we'll pack in work next week.'

'Sounds good to me Roy. Carry on.'

'Whey, we'll tek a months sabbatical - or until we run out of brass. Mek ower way back to England via frogland. Sneak aboard a lorry at one of the ports - preferably one full o' booze. Jump out at Dover where we'll be tekken to be interviewed.'

'They'll sus us out straightaway man.'

'Ah . . . now that's where my cunning plan comes into play.'

'What plan?'

'Easy . . . "We no speaker the English. We Russian" - Because our skin colour is similar. They'll not gan into detail, they're far too busy. Under-staffed. Mek up a name like Ivor Bollokoff or summat else Russian sounding. Nee one'll cotton on we're tekking the piss. Try an' explain to the custom divvies in broken English that we escaped from a political prison in Siberia where we were bummed every neet by sadistic guards. They'll not inspect your rectum unless we're unfortunate an' cop fer a bum bandit custom geezer. Then it'll be the old Marigold gloves an' a tub of axel grease up the jacksey.'

'I'm ganning off this idea rapidly,' squirmed Billy.

'Divent sweat man. It'll be a piece o' piss.'

'It's a piece of brown stuff I'm worried aboot.'

'That was just an extreme example. It'll never 'appen. We'll be handed a wad of cash an' taxied to the nearest five star hotel where we'll reside for a year or two until ower false claims are processed. The British government are good that way - not rushing things. They like to be very thorough in getting their facts correct. In the meantime, all being well, we'll get a bit of work on the side. Cash in hand of course. Back at the Hilton we'll knob all the fit chambermaids - plus the old dogs in your case, cos ar nar yer not ower fussy. Give the waitresses a good seeing to . . . Job's a good un - No worries mate,' ended Roy in his best, but poor Australian accent.

'Sounds a good plan yer've worked out Roy, apart from the 'old dog' chambermaids bit. Count me in.'

'Good lad. Yer nar it meks sense. So, that's ower future mapped out then. We'll hand our notice in first thing Monday morning. Okay . . . the firm'll gan bust but - Hey, that's life! Or as a Frenchman would say, "J'ai cessè de fumer."'

'An what's that mean in English?'

'I have given it up. Put it there pal,' said Roy offering his hand to Billy who duly shook it. 'Wicked man, wicked,' reacted Roy excitedly. 'Ar just wish ar'd thought o' this a couple o' years back. All that shite ale we've put up wi' down at the Phoenix could've been avoided. Ower livers an' other major organs wouldn't be so damaged. Remind me to sue John in the immediate future.'

'On what premise like?' asked Billy.

'Slowly poisoning us with the chemical fuelled witch-piss he passes off as beer. It's time he was brought to book. Ar've kept shtum fer far too long. An' while I'm at it, ar'll sue that chinky tekaway.'

'The chinky? How come?'

'Fer clogging ower arteries by means of unidentified animal fats. Also digestion deterioration through serving unfresh crustaceans. In fact, ar'll throw in crustacean cruelty while I'm at it. This time next year bonny lad, we'll be millionaires.'

'What, like MPs yer mean?'

'No Billy, divent be so silly. We winna be that rich. When ar've got some readies accumulated an' a pile of brown envelopes - what's known in the trade as 'a bunch of Hamiltons' - then ar'll grease a few palms - nudge nudge, wink wink. Nar what ar mean? Mebbe by the time I'm in me mid twenties I'll 'ave set the poilitical wheels in motion. It'll be well worth it mind . . . a ridiculously high salary . . . Even greater expenses - claim fer all sorts . . . Lobby on behalf of a few companies, who in turn'll reward you with a directorship or the like. You turn up an' show yer face a couple of times a year. Tek the brown envelope an' yer laughing all the way to your off-shore account . . . Come here, there's more,' beckoned Roy. 'You'll also get a fantastic guaranteed pension for life - unlike all the other poor ripped off masses. You winna have to stretch the old grey matter neither. Yer'll be permanently on message - told what to do an' say. There is a down side o' course, but only a minor one . . . Yer'll have a small chip inserted somewhere on your person. Yer'll be a kind of robot with spin facilities. But, having said that Billy boy - you only have to work eighty-seven days a year. Admittedly, you may have to attend the odd monthly surgery fer a couple of hours, listening to the public moaning on aboot this an' that. Just look sincere an' tell 'em yer'll look into whatever piffling grievances they've got the nerve to bother you with. Then, show them the exit - instantly forgetting aboot them and their problems. It'll be brilliant man. All that power an' money . . . an' yer'll get more freebie holidays than Judith Chalmers. Yer canna go wrong.'

'An' what political party would you stand for in the local an' general elections?'

'It doesn't matter really . . . Probably the one that looks most likely to win ar suppose. After all, at the end of the day, they all piss in the same pot. Personally, my eventual aim is to become President of Europe - not unlike ower present prime minister, and, like him, I will carry on licking American VIPs arses - Spread my wings so to speak. You canna have too many influential friends. Contacts are paramount in politics. Let's be reet chaps, it's not what yer nar, but who yer nar.'

117

'Whey, that's true,' said Stuart.

'Aye, it'll never change,' added Billy.

'Anyway, that's all in the future,' stated Roy. 'For now, ar'll just keep mekking the odd donation to the BNP. Ar'll keep it all clandestine obviously. Ar divent want to blot the old copy book fer when ar stand to be an MP - the first fleeting rung on the ladder of my inevitable rise to the top. Oh yes . . . tek it from me gentlemen, ar've got it all sussed out. Nee problem.'

Roy nonchalantly sipped his beer, waiting for Alistair's predictable backlash. After all, that was the real intention of his little staged political broadcast. The truth be known, politics bored Roy rigid, but of late, there seemed to be no escaping the current topical subject. Especially the outrageous shenanigans of the present government - the biggest imbeciles to ever run a country, or to be more precise - ruin a country. Like it or not, political affairs hit Roy, as it does most people from all directions. Front page of the daily newspapers, television, and radio etc. constantly updating or, more often, repeating the latest snippet of news, and then exaggerated by the tabloids to sell more copies. All this contributed to heated debates down the Phoenix. Roy viewed it all pragmatically. If you can't beat 'em, join 'em. So why not rant and rave to evoke Alistair's wishy-washy liberal stances on most subjects and have some fun at the same time? Having never doubted it on this occasion, it had worked.

'That's a typical far right bigoted view that the British National party thrive on!' seethed Alistair. 'And the tabloids have a lot to answer for, stirring up trouble regarding the asylum seekers. The Tories are just as bad, jumping on the bandwagon. Making Draconian statements on the whole asylum seeking debate. They've no compassion! They're just desperate for votes from any quarter. Desperation is a word that readily comes to mind concerning that leader-less disorganised bunch of losers. No compassion, none of 'em!'

'Ar've just had a thought,' piped up Roy.

'Now, there's a novelty,' skitted Stuart.

'Shut it you. As ar was trying to say before Milky interrupted me. When Blair gets ower currency changed - an' let's not kid our sens, we'll 'ave a say in it - But will Poundstretcher be called Eurostretcher? It's a consideration, yer must admit.'

'Trust you,' chuckled Billy.

'I lie awake every neet wondering the exact same thing,' said Stuart. 'In my opinion MPs are like babies nappies.'

'An' how d'yer mek that out?'

'Because Billy, they're full of shit an' should be changed regularly.'

There were mutual nods of agreement with the exception of Alistair who remained stoic looking. He was now in fact fretting at the thought of his girlfriend meeting his brash, unpredicatble cousin. Billy had noticed and decided to engage him in conversation, any conversation.

"Ave yer got yer lottery numbers on Alistair?'

'No chance Billy. I won't do it out of principle,' replied Alistair.

'How d'yer mean like?'

'Because most of the tickets are bought by northern people, but the bulk of the funds are spent down south.'

'For instance?'

'Opera houses, the arts, twelve million for the Churchill papers - whatever they are. That Millennium Dome fiddle. There were plenty of fingers in that pie an' all pocketing some serious money. Millions of peoples money ripped off. Did you know there's more than three point two billion pounds - yes billions, in unspent lottery money? It's scandalous.'

'Oh no, he's off on another one already,' chuntered Roy to Stuart. 'The first lecture of many more no doubt,' he added.

'Dur . . . Says you who's not stopped lecturing all morning yer hypocrite,' pointed out Stuart. 'You just love getting your Alistair ganning.'

'Moi? Never,' smirked Roy, his nose suddenly and inexplicably sniffing the air.

'What yer sniffing?'

'Ar can smell pussy Stewpot.'

'Here we go again,' sighed Stuart.

'Ye may mock, but my snout is like radar when it comes to beaver.'

'Give ower man, it'll be your sweaty scrotum.'

'Oh, ye of little faith. Tek a butcher's fer yer sen then Milky. There's three canny looking lasses heading in ower direction. Watch an' learn sonny, the master's at work.'

'Ar canna wait,' sighed Stuart.

Roy greeted the unsuspecting trio, 'Good afternoon ladies. There's three drinks with your names on them in there, so if you'd like to tek a seat they'll be with you momentarily bonny lasses.'

'Thank, but no thanks, we're in a hurry,' came the abrupt but polite reply from one of the girls.

'Are yer sure? Ha way pet, an' tek the weight off yer feet fer a while,' pleaded Roy.

'You heard her. We're in a rush. What part of "no" don't you understand Taffy?' said another of the girls as they carried on through the alley.

Roy was more than a little miffed and shouted after them, 'For your information I'm not a Taffy! An' by the way . . . Yer wanna spend yer giros on some decent clothes! Eeh by gum!'

Without turning, the same girl raised her arm in the air, giving the finger to Roy.

'And the same to you!' he retaliated. 'Yorkshire slappers,' he muttered. 'Did yer see the state of 'em close up? Faces like smacked arses, the lot of 'em.'

Billy and Stuart were laughing their socks off. Why Roy put himself through this humiliation so often was a mystery only he could answer. He was so thick-skinned, humility was alien to him.

Arthur chastised him for shouting so loud in public and Roy was temporarily subdued, speaking at normal volume, but only for a short time. He just couldn't help himself.

Chapter 7

'What's happened to the old boys?' asked Frank, looking about the immediate vicinity.

'They'll probably be arguing the toss at the bar, insisting they've been short changed or not got a full pint,' surmised Don. 'Ar'll bet any money on it.' Setting off to check out his theory, he almost reached the pub door as it swung open and the old boys traipsed out single file, their faces askance.

'By heck, they nar how to charge fer a pint in Yorkshire, ar'll give 'em that,' bemoaned a po-faced Fred. 'Ar thought I was back in the Phoenix fer a minute there,' he skitted. 'Then ar tasted the ale an' knew straight away ar wasn't.'

'It isn't that inferior,' bluffed John. 'You must 'ave got a duff pint old boy, mine's like nectar,' he goaded knowing full well Fred meant the opposite of his proclamation.

Roy closed in for one of his puckish wind-ups. 'Ar thought ye old dinosaurs had got lost. Did yer 'ave trouble getting served on account of been ower scruffy? If it's any help to yers, ar noticed an "help the decrepit" shop near the market. Yer wanna tek yer sens down there an' get kitted out. Ar divent like saying it, but them threadbare rags yer wearing are showing the rest of us up. 'Ave yer nee pride?'

'Listen to the catalogue man - Mr Grattan himself. Ar've seen better dressed scarecrows,' hit back Alf.

'Anyway, what's with the hat Andy Capp?' asked Alistair.

'Aye, yer look a reet prat,' added Tom.

'Sez him wi' the Roy Cropper cast-offs,' sneered Roy, referring to Alistair. 'Ave yer been to a Weatherfield jumble sale or summat? All yer need now is a shopping bag an' purse. Oh . . . an' a bloke in tow with his balls chopped off, preferably called Hayley. What ar've seen of Leeds there's any amount of charity shops,' he exaggerated.

'Do they still wear flares an' tank tops in Stanhope then?' skitted Alistair.

'Ar'll 'ave ye nar, we are at the cutting edge of fashion and technology in the north east. Far more advanced than Yorkshire. And for your information, we buy our exclusive clothing from Newcastle or Durham. Designer gear o' course . . . Kelvin Klein, Gucci, Armani . . . '

'That'll be the Armani an' Navy Stores will it?'

'Very droll Yorky.'

'Stanhope at the cutting edge,' laughed Alistair. 'I've heard it all now. You still 'ave the Ku Klux Klan an' a ducking stool.'

'Well, your info is out of date Yorky, cos we've suspended the Ku Klux Klan until further notice. We canna get rid of the ducking stool though - there's too many witches to go at.'

'Aye, that's true,' agreed Alistair. 'Yer've got more than your fair share of bigots, that's for sure.'

'God's strewth! We actually agree on something. Break out the champagne.' Roy's attention was diverted, 'Look at the babylons on that!' he exclaimed in lowered tones as he ogled a well develpoed young lady. 'Ar could bash the bishop ower her, nee problem.'

Alistair shook his head in resignation, not for the first time and certainly not for the last.

Billy had a mischievous glint in his eye - a roguish persona taking hold, which was not uncommon on these outings. Some times he chose to encourage "Roy's World" just for the hell of it.

'Hoy! Roy!'

'Yes Billy Boy?'

'Tell me, do yer practice safe sex?'

I certainly do kidder. Whoever I'm slipping a large portion to at the time - ar put a muzzle on 'em. It stops 'em biting me in their ecstasy. Yer canna be too careful these days. I'd definitely endorse safe sex every time. Muzzle the bitches, that's my motto. The government should set up an advertising campaign - "Listen to Roy Osborne - the man who knows. Practice safe sex every time - Muzzle the bitches. You canna be too careful. Distributed by Osborne Enterprises www.safeknobbing.com"

Frank was returning from the bar with drinks for his little clique. He gratefully accepted the help of another customer as he struggled through the door with the tray of pints. 'Ar took the liberty of buying you another pint Joseph, did I do reet? You'll be staying fer a meal won't you?'

'Ar will Frank. Cheers. This'll be the last pint of the day fer me mind. Ar'll gan on the soft drinks from now on.'

'Ar should hope so, we divent want a pissed driver,' teased Dennis.

'I tek it yer'll be off on yer usual sight-seeing tour after lunch?' questioned Don.

'Whey, seeing as ar canna stay an' get blathered wi' you lot, the answer is yes. Not that I'm ower bothered like . . . quite the opposite. As yer nar, I'm in me element staking out the local attractions. I never get bored. It's what works fer me. I'm not unfamiliar wi' Leeds either so ar won't be wandering aboot aimlessly.'

'You're wasted on driving buses yer nar,' proclaimed Dennis.

'Can yer put that in writing to show our lass?'

'Nee problem, bonny lad.'

'Sorry to change the subject, but you'll remember the Market Tavern pub won't you Joseph?' asked Arthur reflectively.

'I'll say. Once visited, never forgotten. Ar wouldn't say it was a rough pub, but if you didn't 'ave a black eye, a broken nose or a cauliflower ear - the bouncers wouldn't let you in,' laughed Joseph.

'Aye,' confirmed a staid looking Arthur. 'To say it was rough is a bit of an understatement. Kate Adie was barmaid an' John Prescott was on the door. Customers left their weapons in the cloakroom an' collected 'em on the way out!'

'I remember the Market Tavern,' chipped in John. 'A brilliant boozer. It served a great pint. Granted, it had a bit of a reputation but ar never encountered any trouble on any of my visits. In fact, ar met some colourful characters in there. Great company,' he reflected.

'I always sat by the window,' stated Joseph.

'Oh aye, why's that like?'

'Because the glass was bulletproof! No, joking aside John, ar never experienced any bother either. I tell yer what, ar'd no need to gan shopping when ar lived here in the eighties. You could get everything in the Tavern. There was more traders in there than in Kirkgate Market. Aye, it was some pub that. Once I got to nar the reet people ar got many a bargain.'

'Eeh . . . yer nowt but a fence Joseph Haynes.'

'Aye, me an' a thousand others. Serves the stores an' shops reet fer ower charging us.'

'These public houses wi' the old characters are a dying breed,' pondered John. 'A lot o' pubs get bad names, unjustifiably in a lot of cases. I've been in the licensed trade many a year an' nar what's ganning on. Ar mean . . . you have these pubs with so-called "hard men" in them, but that doesn't mean they're confrontational all the time - only when it's called for. Let's say fer instance, a paedophile or someone that batters old folks, they'd be sorted out big time, an' rightly so in my view. These namby-pamby judges divent give a toss aboot the victims. They bend ower backwards to molly-coddle the scum that do these horrendous crimes . . . letting 'em off with a slapped wrist, free to go after their next victim . . . A word in the right ear can result in proper justice, and I fer one 'ave nee problem with that. An eye for an' eye and all that.'

'Ar'll not disagree wi' that,' said Arthur, nodding his approval.

'It's round aboot this time of day I usually tek me power nap,' declared Roy, yawning with embellishment, looking at his watch. 'But there's nee chance of that among this noisy Yorkshire rabble.'

'Power nap my arse,' derided Billy. 'What he really means is that he 'as a nap at work every afternoon - unless the gaffer's aboot.'

'Trouble with you ginna, is you're not familiar with modern day working practices. It's been overwhelmingly proven by many individual sleep organisations worldwide, that executive stress . . '

'Executive stress!'

'That's what ar said.'

'You 'ave to be an executive before succumbing to "executive stress,"' stated Billy.

' I was giving an example, that's all. Like I was saying . . . it has been proven, that partaking of fifteen minutes slumber, mid afternoon, recharges one's batteries. Therefore, being revitalised, one ups their work load by as much as thirty per cent. Very beneficial to the company, no doubt. You'll 'ave noticed my energy burst come the afternoon.'

'As if.'

'Yer must be in denial Billy.'

'Denial my arse. The only energy you use after your afternoon kip is stretching, yawning an' looking at yer watch every two minutes until home time.'

'Yer divent grasp the conceptualization of what I'm trying to convey to you. Power napping is not just for extra physical stamina - the benefits gan further. It also aids concentration of the mind. Ar can understand how it might look to a retard like yer sen - an ar divent mean that in a derogatory way,' patronised Roy.

'What a load of tripe.'

'I assure you it's not. Ar'll admit, it may look to you that I'm skiving, but nothing could be further from the truth.'

'You wouldn't nar the truth if it hit you in the face.'

'Now, there's no need to cast aspersions on my integrity bonny lad. It's only a matter of my superior brain taking an in depth perspective on whatever current assignment we may be working on at the time. Seeing the big picture - yer might say. Looking to the end result. Perfection every time.'

'What a Paul Anka,' muttered Stuart.

'You can say that again,' agreed Alistair.

'Yeah yeah, I get the so-called "big picture"' sniped Billy, 'Enough bull, let's change the subject afore ar lose the will to live. Four more pints coming reet up,' he said heading off in the direction of the bar.

'Ha way Alistair, get supping. You're lagging behind,' cajoled Roy.

'Don't sweat, I'll keep up with yer,' said Alistair positively, but hiding his reservations all the same.

'Billy'll be ages in there.'

'Why d'yer say that Royston?' asked Stuart.

'Cos he'll be nipping to the bog fer a quick smoke of one o' them Moroccan Woodbines.'

'Is he on dope?' exclaimed Alistair in surprise.

'Ar doubt it Ali,' Stuart reassured him. 'We were down Crook on a pub crawl one neet last month an' Billy was legless. Anyway, to cut to the chase, best I could mek out of the tale was that an old mate of Billy's had let him have a few blows of a spliff in the bog. Billy canna remember a thing aboot it, but yer nar how wind-up Roy likes to elaborate on these stories. Most lads 'ave tried a bit of grass - it's part of growing up. Personally, when I tried it a couple of years back, it did nowt fer me. I'm happy to stick with the beer an' the occasional short.'

'Aye, me too.'

''Ave ye not tried any drugs Alistair?' Stuart asked. 'They must be rife in a big city like Leeds.'

'Can't say I have.'

'Is it against yer religion or principles?' Roy goaded his younger cousin.

'Right first time,' said Alistair adamantly.

'Ar thought as much.'

'Nowt wrong wi' that.'

'Ar never said there was.'

'Drugs are for mugs.'

'Hey up! A poet to boot our Alistair!'

'That's me.'

'You were quick,' said a surprised Stuart as Billy placed a tray of beer on the table.

'Ar divent mess aboot bonny lad,' boasted Billy. 'The young fit barmaids almost came to blows over who would have the pleasure of serving this fine specimen of a man stood before you now. Fortunately the manager was on duty and stepped in before I was

126

ravaged. They were like wild animals. I kid you not.'

'Bollocks,' scoffed Roy.

'Listen to kettle calling pot black for a change,' smirked Billy.

'Your tables are ready gentlemen,' informed a smart, well spoken dickey-bowed waiter, having just stepped out of the luncheon rooms to address the old boys, John, and the rest of the dining party. They didn't need telling twice. By this time ravenous, they followed with a spring in their step. Indeed, the waiter could be forgiven in thinking a sudden hurricane had manifested itself as he held the door open allowing them to enter.

Old Tom, the last one through grumbled to Alf, 'If he thinks he's getting a tip fer holding a door oppen, he's got another think coming.'

'Ooh no, perish the thought. Yer canna brek the habit of a lifetime at your age now,' smiled Alf

'Ar hope you're not insinuating I'm a bit tight lad.'

'As if, Tom. Thou offendeth me.'

'Sit down yer big daft sod,' guffawed old Tom, giving him a gentle shove in the back.

'Ar wonder if they'll cope with their grub,' said Roy.

'How'd yer mean like?' asked Stuart.

'Whey, beacause they use knives an' forks in there.'

'Yer don't say.'

'Yeah, it surprised me too. Knives and forks in Yorkshire - what next?'

'There's a couple of birds heading this way,' stated Billy.

'Where we looking?' asked Stuart.

'Coming up the alley here. I'm sure one of 'em's waving at me.'

'Divent talk soft man, she's waving at me,' insisted Roy.

'Don't get over excited you lot,' said Alistair, hardly daring to breathe with apprehension.

'Why not Yorky?'

'Because the one waving is my girlfriend Janet, and the other's her sister.'

'Whey, ar never,' exclaimed a bemused Billy.

'It's true. I arranged to meet up here with them for a drink, though God knows why,' sighed Alistair.

Momentarily, and it was momentarily unfortunately - Roy was speechless. Gobsmacked. He soon recovered. 'Are you being serious or what?' he asked.

'Course I am,' confirmed Alistair, pensively thinking to himself, whatever possessed him to arrange to meet Janet here in the same vicinity as the Weardale foghorn?

'Whey, aren't you the dark horse? An' there was I, certain yer batted fer the other side,' smirked Roy disparagingly.

'Another original Osborne quote, I think not,' hit back Alistair.

Roy took a comb from his pocket, spat on it and ran it through his hair.

'Urgh . . . yer jacket's covered in dandruff now,' teased Stuart.

'It isn't is it?' said Roy, checking his shoulders relieved to find them unblemished.

'Hah . . . daft fer looking dick-head.'

'Grow up Milky, yer big kid.'

'Talking of big kids, try an' act like a grown-up Roy,' pleaded Alistair.

'Divent sweat man, ar'll just be me sen.'

'That's what I'm worried about.'

'Relax kidder. Ar'll be too busy chatting up your bird's sister to cause havoc.'

'Don't bother, she's spoken for an' all.'

'Correction - was spoken for. She'll drop him like a lead balloon once the old Royston charm kicks in.'

Alistair shook his head in resignation. What the hell - go with the flow. A few more pints would soon disseminate Roy's appalling brashness. The thought entered Alistair's head, which he'd later ask the opinion of others - but was it only him that deliberated the fact that Roy Osborne and Coronation Street's Les Battersby must have been separated at birth? If the nuclear button was pressed and the world was minutes from obliteration, he envisaged the pair propping up the Rover's Return bar dismissing it as a minor occurrence. Each with a pint in their hand, boasting of their next conquest, with lashings of spin as was their norm. Surely the excuses that passed themselves off as our political parties had missed out on two of Britain's finest spinners.

128

'Bonjoir mademoiselles.'

'Hello,' greeted Janet. 'Don't tell me - you're Roy Osborne.'

'The very same, fair young maiden. I see my reputation precedes me. And you are, if I may enquire?'

'I'm Janet and this is my sister Linda.'

'Pleased to meet you both I'm sure,' creeped Roy, shaking their hands before introducing them to Stuart and Billy.

The sisters were very similar in looks. Both were a petite five foot two or three inches and they each had brunette shoulder length hair.

'You must be the short-sighted one Janet,' declared Roy.

'An' how d'yer mek that out?'

'Cos yer'd 'ave to be, to gan out with ower Alistair,' chortled Roy.

'Ha ha, that would have been funny if I were still at primary school,' said Janet with derision, much to the delight of everyone present.

It bothered Roy not one jot, quite the opposite in fact. 'Yer a spunky lot ye Yorkshire lasses, ar'll give yer that much.'

'Aye, we are that lad. We're made o' sturdy mettle aren't we big sis?' said Janet in an exaggerated Yorkshire dialect.

'Tha's not wrong little sis,' agreed a very self-assured Linda. 'We can even deal wi' trouble int' mill if needs be.'

'I love it!' laughed Roy.

'Take a seat girls,' offered Alistair as he and Billy vacated theirs. 'Two halves of Stella is it?' he asked, already knowing their tipple.

'Yes please,' the sisters echoed.

'Coming right up,' he said cheerfully, feeling more relaxed now the introductions were over.

'How long have you known Alistair then?' asked Billy.

'About three months now,' pondered Janet.

'Where did yer meet him? If I'm not being too nosy.'

'No, there's no secret. We met in a pub.'

'Whey yer dee surprise me,' piped up Roy.

'An' why's that?' questioned Janet.

'I'm not being funny, but ar'd of guessed that yer'd met in a library or some other academic building.'

'Why would yer think that?'

'Whey, wi' 'im being a boffin like.'

'I can see where you're coming from. He is a bit studious. He's even writing a novel at the moment. But I can assure you he does find the time to socialise, otherwise I'd never have met him on a night out, would I?'

'Never mind pet, you were just unlucky. Wrong time, wrong place.'

'I'm not complaining.'

'Fair do's. He's a canny lad mind.' Roy leaned closer to Janet. 'But between me and you, ar wouldn't believe a word he tells yer. He lives in his own little world.'

'That's funny, cos Alistair said exactly the same about you. And no offence *pet*, but I'm more inclined to believe him.'

Billy and Stuart were thoroughly enjoying the banter. This Yorkshire lass gave as good as she got and they loved it.

'So, do yer both live in Leeds then?' asked Stuart.

'Yes, we live in Armley,' replied Linda. 'It's not far. About a mile an' a half from here.'

'Is that where the infamous Armley Jail is?'

'The very same.'

'Divent yer ever worry that some prisoners could escape?'

'Don't be daft. As far as I know there's hardly been any escapes over donkey's years. So why worry?'

'Because you live near the jail.'

'Well, put it this way - If someone escaped, which is highly unlikely - what's the first thing he's gonna do?'

'Find a prostitute an' mek up fer lost time,' suggested Roy.

'Well, he might seek out the services of a lady of the night,' agreed Linda. 'But the first thing he'd do is get as far away from the jail as possible. So he's not gonna be bothering the local residents is he?'

'Yeah, you're reet,' nodded Stuart. 'He'll be off like a bat out of hell.'

'Whey, ar beg to differ,' said Roy.

'You would.'

'Well, give us your take on this hypothetical scenario then,' challenged Janet. 'I can hardly contain myself.'

'Who's a sarky young lady then?' taunted Roy. 'The way ar see it is like this . . . After an hour or so on the run - for the sake of my little saga, let's call the escapee Mr X.'

'That's original,' skitted Janet.

'Just get thee pipe. As I was conveying on this Mr X . . . A short spell of freedom, choking on Leeds polluted air an' getting mugged a couple of times - he'll be knocking on Armley Jail's door, begging to be let back in. They're like holiday camps them places. Not that ar've had the pleasure of her majesties first hand mind.'

'Is he always this full of fictitious high spirits?' asked Linda.

'Nar, sometimes he's asleep,' gibed Stuart.

'How did we wander off on a tangent about Armley Jail?' questioned Janet.

'Who cares. Let's change the subject,' suggested Roy. 'Tell us a bit more aboot yer sens ladies.'

'Like what?' asked Linda.

'Where yer both work, fer instance,' said Roy.

'Leeds,' was Janet's one word answer, deliberately causing Roy to work hard at his attempted dialogue between them.

'Whey, I assumed that,' he chuntered. 'Would you care to elaborate?'

'Not really.'

'Is she always this talkative your younger sister or is she part mute?' he sneered, turning his attentions to Linda. Roy was too pig-headed and thick-skinned to let Janet's deliberate evasiveness get the better of him.

Stuart and Billy said nothing. They were enjoying themselves too much.

'God, it's like pulling teeth. What happened to this so-called Yorkshire hospitality yer hear so much aboot? Or is that just a myth like everything else?'

'That's south Yorkshire,' Linda informed him.

'Silly me. There I was thinking all Yorkshire folk were friendly.'

'Don't be too hard on yourself,' piped up Janet, abandoning her exile as a mute. It's an easy mistake to make.' She then burst into a fit of giggles alongside Linda.

'I knew you were trying to wind me up all along,' insisted Roy, which happened to be true. It took one bull shitter to recognise another.

'I'm sorry,' apologised Janet. 'I've got a warped sense of humour.'

'That's alreet bonny lass, so have I.'

'What was the question you asked?'

'Ar canna remember now, it's that far back.'

'You were asking us where we worked,' Linda reminded them.

'Aye, that was it,' recalled Roy.

Jesting aside, Janet didn't want to come over as a total ignoramous, though she could tell it would take a lot to offend Alistair's devil-may-care cousin who was completely opposite in character to him. Alistair's low-down on Roy wasn't exactly glowing in praise but she couldn't help thinking that at least there would be very few dull moments spent in his company. She did conclude that the novelty value would be short lived though.

'We both work for the same publishing house in the Merrion Centre.'

'Is that central then?'

'Yes, just a five or six minute walk from here.'

'Handy fer shopping then,' said Roy stating the obvious.

'Too handy.'

'How d'yer mean like?'

'It's too convenient. All the shops an' stores on your office doorstep. Too often, you end up looking in them in your lunch hour an' end up buying something you wouldn't if you worked out of town.'

'They don't call it shopping these days, it's called "retail therapy",' Linda pointed out. 'God! I hate that description.'

'Like you hate that one of you?' questioned Janet.

'What are you on about?'

'Shopoholic.'

'Rubbish!'

'It's true,' insisted Janet. 'Go on, tell the lads your nick-name. Let them judge.'

'I'll kill you when we get home,' threatened Linda. 'I may have been referred to as "QVC Linda" on the odd occasion,' she divulged.

'Odd occasion? And the rest!'

'Now, now ladies. Let's not be falling out,' placated Roy. What's QVC stand for anyway?'

Janet obliged, 'Quality, value and covenience.'

'I'm still no wiser,' said Roy.

'It's a shopping channel on the telly. The only channel that exists as far as our lass is concerned.'

'You don't half exaggerate,' said Linda on the defensive. 'While we're on the subject, tell everyone your nickname.'

Billy whispered to Stuart, 'These two are as bad as Roy. Talk aboot the quarrelsome twosome.'

'We're waiting,' persisted Linda.

'Well wait no more. I've no qualms over a silly nickname. It's "Little Miss Emporium."'

'Whey, yer divent gan fer the simple nickname options, ar'll give yer that. Little Miss Emporium . . . ' pondered Roy. 'Don't tell me, is that another shopping channel, pardon me, retail therapy channel then?' asked Roy.

Linda cringed. 'Don't use that analogy.'

'Too late bonny lass. You've handed me the ammunition now.'

'My sister - Little Miss Emporium, collects doll's houses and their multitude of accessories. She never grew up, did you love?' said Linda, leaning over and gently pinching Janet's cheek.

'Correction, I have a doll's house - singular. And I could think of worse hobbies.'

'Too right,' came the unexpected support from Roy but accompanied, as was the norm, with a sting in the tail. 'You need a decent hobby ganning out wi' my boring, skinny cousin.'

'Don't you be talking about my beloved in those derogatory terms,' scolded Janet. 'Not everyone's that fond of loud brash people like someone not a million miles away.'

'I apologise unreservedly,' genuflected Roy with about as much sincerity as Tony Blair. 'I truly didn't know your relationship was so serious,' he added, fishing around.

Janet declined the bait, choosing to leave Roy hanging in the balance.

Alistair was coming out of the pub backwards, opening the door with his backside, a half of lager in each hand and two packets of cheese and onion crisps clenched between his teeth. Having originally bought three halves of Stella, he'd swiftly knocked one back in one go. Nothing wrong with a touch of dutch courage he convinced himself. 'Here we are girls,' he said placing their drinks and crisps on the barrel top table. He squeezed in to sit next to Janet, giving her a quick peck on the cheek. The two girls took a welcome swig of beer, satisfying a thirst that was well overdue.

'Pushing the boat out a bit kidder. Crisps as well?' teased Roy.

'You know me Roy, generous to a fault,' countered Alistair. 'I tell you what, it's like a sardine tin in there. Ruddy chaos.'

'I wondered what took you so long,' remarked Janet.

'That's the only trouble with this pub. Top end's too narrow by far. I tried attracting me grandad's attention through the luncheon room but it was like knitting fog. Too many bodies in the way.'

'Being Saturday afternoon doesn't help,' said Janet.

'That's true.'

'It's great,' enthused Stuart, well pleased with their descent on Leeds. 'All these people milling around. I love the atmosphere. It's exciting - lifts yer spirits.'

'Aye, yer reet,' agreed Billy animatedly, as if Stuart had triggerred off some sort of sedate chain reaction. 'Come to think of it, it's infectious this feeling of collective vitality,' he added taking in the surroundings, nodding and smiling contentedly.

Roy put on his best bemused expression as if to convey this was just another normal day in the life of a cool-cat such as himself. 'Yer must excuse them,' he addressed the two sisters, 'As you'll 'ave obviously gathered by now - several of the Stanhope massive divent get out much.'

'Stop trying to mek out you're some sort of worldly-wise globe-trotter,' berated Stuart. 'Showing off in front of the lasses. Yer aboot as well travelled as a laboratory mouse.'

'Aye, but hold up a mo. Roy's actually said summat constructive fer once. Albeit inadvertently.'

'Like what? Gan on, surprise me Billy.'

'He said we divent get out much.'

'And, point being?'

'Whey, he's right fer a change.'

'Who, motor-mouth there?'

'Hey, watch it lad,' warned Roy.

'If ar could just get my idea across chaps,' pleaded Billy.

'Gan on we're listening,' Stuart assured him.

'Whey, it's like Roy said, a couple of trips a year isn't enough. We need to get ower heads together. Get round the table back home sometime, and organise more outings.'

'Sounds good to me,' agreed Stuart.

'Excellent idea Ginna. Count me in,' said Roy. 'Anything to get away from home. We'll 'ave a word with the walking dead in the near future but fer now, I'm only interested in today. Cheers!' Roy raised his glass and took a gulp.

'Whey, what happened to this great European expedition you an' Billy were ganna embark upon after yer'd handed yer notice in on Monday?' asked Stuart.

'Whey, we winna be gone forever! We're not intending to emigrate - except back into Britain when the brass runs out, like ar telt yer earlier. Stop being so negative man.'

Stuart finished his beer. 'Same again everyone?' he invited getting up from his seat.

The sisters looked at one another, each in two minds.

'Go on, why not. Two halves of Stella please,' replied Linda.

'Coming reet up ladies.' Taking a deep breath, Stuart braced himself in readiness to tackle the busy bar.

'What do you and Billy do for a living?' Janet asked Roy.

'As little as possible,' skitted Alistair.

'Ignore him hinny. He's just jealous of my status in life.'

'And what might that be?' probed Janet further.

'To give it it's proper title - I'm an entrepreneur. Fingers in many pies yer nar.'

'Aye, mostly Safeway pork pies, every lunchtime,' scoffed Billy. 'He works with me for a local builder pet. Entrepreneur my backside!'

'Alreet gobshite, ar'll re-phrase that - I'm a future entrepreneur - satisfied?'

'Meks nee odds to me.'

'It will when yer've got yer begging bowl out.'

'All talk as usual. Stop deluding yer sen Royston.'

'We'll see. By the time I'm thirty, ar'll be a billionaire.'

'Dream on bonny lad.'

'Ye may mock, but just wait an' see. Ar'll mek that Richard Branston - '

'Branson,' corrected Billy.

'Whatever. He'll look like a pauper aside o' me.'

'Are you two like this all the time?' asked Linda.

'Aye. Ar tek me personal stereo to work with me though,' stated Billy. When ar canna stand his prattling on, I stick me headphones on. If ar didn't, ar'd end up in the looney bin.'

'Same gans fer me,' sniffed Roy. 'You're not exactly a bag o' laughs to work wi'.'

'What d'yer expect? I always end up doing the work of two men! You just stand aboot like a spare prick at a wedding. Bloody useless.'

'That's the foreman's perocative.'

'Prerogative. And you're not a foreman.'

'I'm the unofficial foreman. Temporarily, until the gaffer's sorted out the paperwork. I wasn't ganna say owt an' spoil your day, but there you are, it's out in the oppen now. Boss had no option but to promote me - I was being head-hunted.'

'Head-hunted! Who by? Cannibals in the Brazilian rainforest?'

'Yer might tek the piss but you'll 'ave to book your ideas up in the future or ar'll be handing you yer cards laddie.'

'Change the subject lads,' pleaded Janet.

'Aye, alreet. Let's dicuss this secret novel our Alistair's supposed to be writing,' said Roy sarcastically. 'What's it gonna be aboot Yorky?'

'Wait an' see. You'll find out when yer buy a copy,' said Alistair smugly. An' don't sweat, I'll reserve you a copy.'

'Typical Yorkshire miser, charging his closest relative. Anyway, when this mystery book is finished how yer ganna get a publisher to tek it on? What little ar nar on the subject ar do know it's nigh impossible getting published.'

'Absolutely. You've hit the nail on the head Roy. That's why I'm self publishing.'

'Can yer do that?'

'Just watch me.'

'Ar've nee doubt you will kidder.'

'Obviously I don't have delusions of becoming a best seller, every man an' his dog have a book out. I've got two chances - slim and none. And slim is not in town,' Alistair accepted.

'Yer wanna write aboot famous people,' advised Billy. 'Loads do it. There's a name for 'em . . . ' he pondered.

'Biographies.'

'That's it Ali.'

'I wouldn't be a biographer for all the tea in China. Parasites, the lot of 'em. Lazy writers . . . They just copy literature regarding famous people. Ten-a-penny, talentless plagiarists.'

'What's a plagiarist when it's at home?' asked Billy.

Alistair enlightened him, 'It's someone who copies somebody elses work.'

'Well, if I were an author, then that's what ar'd be - A playerist,' stated Roy. 'No thinking to dee. Just copy others work. Definitely meks sense to me.'

'Now why doesn't that surprise me?'

'Whey, it's reet . . . Fools an' horses an' all that.'

'Do you do much reading Roy?' asked Janet.

'Now an' again, if I get the chance. I'm always busy. In demand an' all that yer nar.'

'Give ower man,' scoffed Stuart. 'All he ever reads is porn mags from the top shelf.'

'Keep that out Milky,' said Roy tapping his nose. 'I'm having an intellectual conversation with this young lady here. Pray, carry on Janet. I apologise unreservedly on behalf of my moronic colleague.'

'Apology accepted,' chuckled Janet. 'I was going to say - if you got the opportunity to read a book, what type would it be?'

'Whey, ar never bother wi' trashy novels an' the like. Ar'd go fer

137

informed literary reading. Philosophy . . . books in that category.'

The lads looked at each other, shaking their heads at Roy's bullshit as Janet carried on the charade.

'Have you any words of wisdom you can share with us at this moment Roy?'

'Let me think bonny lass . . . I have many phraseology snippets to gan at.' Roy rubbed his chin and pondered a while, 'Aye, I've got one for yer.' He coughed and cleared his throat, 'Confucius say . . . "Man with hands in pocket feels cocky all day." Will that do yer pet?'

'Yes, very profound. I suppose it's the nearest I'll get to a straight answer from you,' said Janet with a chuckle.

'Whey, I'm not just a pretty face yer nar. In all seriousness though, ar have read the odd book. An SAS book by Andy McNab was the last one - Zero summat or other - aboot his an' his team's exploits behind enemy lines in the first Gulf War. It was alreet - the usual exaggerated macho bullshit. My reading normally stretches nee further than the daily tabloids. I tek 'em wi' a pinch o' salt mind. They seem to compete for the biggest bullshit award story of the day.'

'He's here is the lad,' announced Billy clearing several glasses to one side of the table.

Stuart set the heavy tray of drinks down with relief. 'Phew! It's like an oven in there,' he said wiping the sweat from his brow with the back of his hand.

'It'll be all that hot air those Yorkshire punters are spouting,' sneered Roy.

They all thanked Stuart and gulped their drinks having by now "got the taste." Any remaining inhibitions were now rapidly evaporating in the jovial surroundings.

'Are you sure these drinks are not spiked?' suggested Linda, 'because I feel quite tiddly already.'

'It must be you our lass, because I feel fine.'

'You're probably right sis, I'm drinking on an empty stomach. I only had half a piece of toast at Steve's an' that was hours ago. How about you?'

'That's a daft question. It's not that long since you left home. I had my usual full monty like every other weekend.'

'Ooh! Get You! Beam me up Snotty.'

'Tell Steve to get some grub in, yer'll be wasting away. Mind you, yer can't get much food in that fridge, it's full of cans of beer. An' the larders no better - stocked to the ceiling with thousands of smuggled cigarettes.'

'Stop having a go at my Steve. And for your information, there was a can of Netto beans and sausages I could have had but I wasn't hungry.'

'I'm not having a go, it's just that I think he could take a leaf from Alistair's book.'

'What leaf's that then?'

'Where to begin . . . He doesn't smoke, only drinks occasionally. He attends midnight mass every Christmas Eve. I could go on.'

Alistair winked at the bemused lads. He was obviously used to these sisterly spats.

'I'd watch her Alistair.'

'An' why's that Linda?'

'Because if you're not careful she'll 'ave a ring on her finger an' you'll be up the aisle before you know it. An' once she's got you shackled yer'll be forced to sign-up to the Temperance movement.'

'What's that when it's at home?'

'In short - a group of dollards who believe in abstinence from alcohol and controlling ones appetites and desires.'

'Take no notice love. She's only jealous of your chivalry towards me - your better half,' teased Janet, giving Alistair a cuddle.

'Linda, there's a bag of crisps on the table. Get them down yer neck. It'll help soak up the beer,' suggested Alistair.

'Oh yeah, I forgot. I must be pissed,' giggled Linda.

'Language our lass!'

'Oh, f . . . fiddlesticks!' dismissed Linda.

'Whey, yer speak my language pet,' smarmed Roy. 'Yer growing on me by the minute. Yer better off without that selfish boyfriend by the sound of it. Come home wi' me pet. Ar've got a tin o' Heinz beans an' sausages. None of that cheap Netto crap.'

'Here we go,' sighed Alistair. 'More bullshit's inevitable.'

'Linda, you've got beautiful blue eyes. I could live in them.'

'You can. I've got a stye in one of them.'

Everyone was in stitches but Linda's retort didn't deter Roy.

'Great joke lass, are yer sure we're not related?'

'Positive "bonny lad".'

'We could be.'

'Pass.'

'Yer divent nar what yer missing pet. I wasn't called Roy the fox at school fer nowt yer nar.'

'Why was that then? Cos you're sly and cunning?'

'Nar. It was because any birds that chased him were dogs,' chipped in Stuart.

'Very droll. Ar thought you'd nodded off milky boy.'

'I'm wide awake and raring to go. Divent you worry aboot that.'

'Ar winna,' said Roy, returning his attention to the girls. 'So, what yer deeing fer the rest of the day? What's on the agenda after yer've hired the pick-up truck?'

'Why would we need a pick-up truck?' asked Janet.

'Whey, it's obvious.'

'Not to me it isn't.'

'To carry all them carrier bags yer've got tucked away in the corner there. Let's 'ave a butchers,' said Roy, examining the girls shopping. 'What we got . . . ? Marks an' Sparks, House o' Fraser, Debenhams, Allders, River Island, Harvey Nicks, Bhs, Boots, TKMax, Bodycare, HMV, Virgin, Waterstones, Borders, Next, Warehouse, Dorothy Perkins . . .'

'Alright, you can stop now, we've got your gist. I'm impressed. How d'you remember all them big store names when we've only got bags from eight of 'em?'

'A secret closet shopper, eh Roy?' suggested Billy.

'Nar, you're way off the mark laddie. There's nee mystery. They're names whose ruddy adverts regularly tek up half my daily newspaper. Hang on a minute, ar've just spotted another bag.'

'Where?' asked LInda.

'Here, in the middle of the others,' said Roy, rummaging about in the girls shopping.

'Liar.'

'I'm not. It's an Anne Summers bag. That'll belong to you Janet I presume.'

'And why would you presume that? If it existed,' asked Janet.

'Whey, ar suppose you'll be in need of a few "aids" while yer ganning out with ower Alistair, until you progress to a real man,' he smirked.

'Get stuffed,' retorted Alistair. 'You're just jealous.'

'He is all man, let me tell you that "bonny lad",' insisted Janet, putting her hand on Alistairs knee, leaning over and kissing him on the cheek. Alistair grinned like a Cheshire cat.

'Give ower will yer? grimaced Roy.

'Give over what?' questioned Alistair.

'All that mushy, kissy kissy lark. It puts me off me ale.'

'Tough luck Geordie,' taunted Alistair, who reciprocated Janet's kiss with a smacker on the lips.

Having satisfied his appetite, Joseph had left the confines of the dining room and joined the party outside.

Roy led the introductions, 'Linda, Janet, this is our personal chauffeur, Joseph.'

'Pleased to meet you ladies,' Joseph greeted them warmly.

The sisters responded with a nod and a smile.

'Take no heed of him, I'm the reluctant driver more like.'

'Give ower man,' objected Roy. 'Yer mek a fortune out of us.'

'You must be joking. If ar didn't half inch me fuel from the works depot, I'd be out o' pocket! Just joking ladies.'

'Liar. He syphons off all his personal fuel.'

'I get a discount Roy. There's a big difference.'

'He'll tell us owt.'

'It's true . . . By the way, your granda's found a soul-mate in the eatery.'

'What d'yer mean?'

'He's in deep conversation an' down memory lane with another like-minded chap, regards Leeds United's golden years.'

'That'll be a short discussion then,' skitted Roy. 'I wasn't aware they had any so called "golden years".'

'They certainly did!' responded Alistair. 'We weren't always crap like nowadays,' he said in all frankness. 'But I don't think you're in a position to knock anyone.'

'An' why's that Yorky?'

'Two words Royston - Sunderland. Relegation. I rest my case.'

'That's irrelevant bollock chops.'

'How come?'

'Because ar divent support them losers anymore.'

'Since when?'

'Since they got relegated,' interjected Billy. 'Reckons he's changed his allegiance to Man United.'

'It's a free world.'

'Well that's debatable, but I digress,' said Alistair. 'A true football fan would follow their team through thick and thin. It's too easy to change support to a team that's nearly always on top.'

'Oh, ar divent nar, it seems sensible to me,' declared an unrepentant Roy.

'It's treason man!' said Billy, angrily. Billy was a life-long supporter of Newcastle United despite the teams ups and downs. 'No self-respecting north easterner would ever admit to supporting that Man U scum. Only a moronic arsehole . . . mind you - enough said.'

'Nobody's mentioned Bradford City,' remarked Linda.

'Why would they? Yer scraping the bottom of the barrel now,' derided Roy. 'You are tekking the urine aren't yer? What division are they in? Two or three? Go on, refresh my memory can you pet?'

'The first division!' snapped Linda. 'Same division as Sunderland "pet".'

'Meks nee odds to me. Not my problem.'

'Turncoat. Bradford can't be that bad, my boyfriend follows them.'

'What's his name? Stevie Wonder?'

'Well, he is called Steve.'

'Never mind, someone's got to support 'em I suppose.'

'He doesn't *have* to, he *wants* to.'

'Are yer sure he's not down some lapdance club wi' his mates, using Bradford City as a cover story? That'd explain a lot.'

'Rubbish! He's got me. That's all he needs.'

'Right, I'll love you and leave you,' announced Joseph. 'Enjoy yer sens an' keep out of trouble.'

'Are you off on one of your notable cultural walkabouts of one of the finest cities in the world,' inquired Alistair with assured frivolity.'

'Yer not too far off the mark there Alistair lad.'

'Gan an' shite yer pair o' bullshitters,' scorned Roy, not unexpectedly. 'That honour gans to Newcastle wi' out a doubt.' He cocked a snoop. 'I'd watch these two Janet.'

'What for?'

'Whey, 'ave yer not heard 'em? The pair of uphill gardeners.'

'Uphill gardeners? I'm not with you Roy,' frowned Janet.

'Woolly woofters . . . ' he muttered. 'Bum bandits - yer nar . . . '

'I wish you'd stop talking in riddles.'

'Please yer sen. If yer canna see the wood fer the trees - fair enough.'

'Don't be late back tonight ye lot. Ten o'clock sharp. Any latecomers get left behind so think on.' Joseph walked the short distance down Turks Head Yard, gave a wave and turned onto busy Briggate. Whistling cheerily he went to the centre of what was originally the road. The crowds were thinner on the ground there. Now pedestrianised, Briggate was a paragon. A more shopper friendly environment could be nothing but a winner. The publics ability to move about more freely up and down Briggate had been well overdue but was now a resounding success. Vehicle free for several years now, the only hazard of being in a traffic accident came from the ever increasing number of disability scooters, many of which were driven by budding 80 year old Michael Schumachers. Shoppers would scatter like skittles to avoid injury from these geriatric scooter operators who were seemingly oblivious to pedestrians. Some sort of sanity test should be enforced prior to being let loose amongst the public in a busy city centre. They may assume capability once seated upon an electric scooter but the absence of a minimal amount of common sense, not least a modicum of eyesight, seemed no barrier to the rental shop. Legislation should begin fortwith. In the meantime a small gesture of goodwill wouldn't go amiss. Perhaps an obligatory first aid box accompanying every scooter charter would not break the bank. One has to have a certain sympathy towards these semi-senile Sterling Moss's. Perhaps if they didn't have to wait ten years on an NHS list for a simple cataract operation there would be far fewer accidents. It could be said that another negative regards this whole bone of contention was the smell of stale piss whizzing past you at thirty miles an hour. No great endorsement of these potential, lethal contraptions. A spray of disinfectant liberally applied to each scooter after every outing would go a long way in eradicating any hygiene concerns. A pack of incontinence pads alongside the first aid box in the little scooter basket - Jobs a good un.

Joseph stood gazing at the well known stores either side of Briggate. Debenhams, Dixons, The Body Shop, McDonalds, Borders Books, the Thorntons and Queens Arcades. Most were taken for granted by regular Leeds shoppers but were a refreshingly pleasant sight for the first time visitor - a mecca for all shoppholics. What a contrast between this - a thriving, bustling, cosmopolitan city and a village high street on a Saturday afternoon. With limited choice of shops and therefore lack of goods, the villagers retail therapy was seriously curtailed. The myth that people were queuing to up sticks and move to the countryside was vastly exaggerated. Especially so in todays consumer led society with village Post Offices, banks, schools, shops and pubs now closed for business, or about to be. A lot of would be adventurers would soon be scurrying back to their more convenient urban lifestyles.

Just before the Headrow, tucked away up a narrow passage (blink and you'd miss it) is the cosy Leeds City Varieties famous for "The Good Old Days" show with Leonard Sachs as the irrepressible chairman. It was televised by the BBC for thirty years finishing in 1983 and breaking all records for a television series. Its popularity never diminished. The live audience of a few hundred dressed in period costume for each show and the waiting list for tickets had reached twenty thousand when the show finally came to a close. A regular haunt for Joseph back in the eighties when he'd worked and lived in the city, he'd spent many a happy hour in the Varieties watching the expansive diversity of acts. His favourite was Johnnie Casson, the brilliantly funny Yorkshire comedian. He chuckled as he recalled one of Johnnie's jokes having seen him on Blackpool's North Pier a couple of years back. "It was that windy in Blackpool today that two Siamese twins were looking for each other" Why he and his ilk were not on television more often was a mystery to Joseph and he wasn't on his own in this opinion. Another favourite of his, Mick Miller regularly appeared in Blackpool. Joseph and his wife Jean would go along and see him at every opportunity as well. Surely something along the lines of the jocular TV show "The Comedians" should be raised from the ashes. God knows, we could all do with a good laugh, more so in todays dangerous and fraught times. British television was a disgrace with its constant repeats of Some Mother's do 'ave 'em, Porridge, 'Allo 'Allo and A Touch of Frost, all of which were shown at peak times such as Saturday night. It's not even necessary to video programmes these days as the same series will be back within a couple of months - some programmes the next day even! Decorating, makeovers, what and what not to wear, DIY, how to go for a shit . . . Endless drivel with every other programme a text or phone-in. TV companies fleecing as much money as possible from short-changed viewers on any trivial pretext. Channel 5 news had a phone-in every night at 7.00pm to vote for what colour socks tomorrows news reader should wear. Phone - blah blah plus 01 for black socks or 02 for green socks or 03 for red socks. Who gives a fuck? Stop trying to milk us through our TV screens. And as for the BBC making money hand over fist from these abysmal phone-ins - why don't the long suffering licence payers benefit? Perhaps we'd be more understanding if we didn't have to fork out £120 plus for the compulsory television licence. A revolt is well overdue.

Music hall theatre days were mostly a thing of the past. Joseph, having read up on Leeds past and present had discovered the city had its fair share when they were in their prime. Harvey Nicholls now stands on the site of the Empire Arcade, formerly the Moss Empire Theatre which opened in 1898. Artists who appeared there included Charlie Chaplin, George Robey and Gracie Fields. In 1931 the Empire was adapted for talking pictures showing Charlie Chaplin's first sound film "City Lights" but the theatre soon returned to variety bills. Closing in February 1961, it was demolished in 1962 making way for the Empire Arcade.

Joseph decided to make his way to the library. He was disappointed to see the Odeon Cinema was now derelict. Most cinemas were now re-sited in out-of-town multi-cinema complexes. As with supermarkets, they were all geared for car owners. Opening as The Paramount in 1932, it became the Odeon in 1940. The huge cinema was equally known for its live shows which included artists such as Judy Garland and The Beatles. It also boasted a Wurlitzer organ which was the fourth largest in Europe but was sold in 1968. The Odeon became a twin cinema in 1969. July 1978 saw a third screen opened and it was launched as a five cinema complex in 1988.

A few yards on Joseph had another surprise. The narrow Headrow entrance to the City Varieties was also closed. So much was changing in so short a time and he'd barely strolled 300 yards. Still, that's life. Nothing stays the same forever. Particularly pertinent in the so called modern day. For better or worse? Well, that depended. Ask the old boys and you'd get a resounding answer of decline. Ask the young 'ens and you'd get the complete opposite. After all, wasn't life always a bed of roses in your youth? The cynicism came later in life.

Chapter 8

'Bah, she's a big Yorkshire lass,' whispered Roy, as a rather rotund young lady went past them. 'Must 'ave been on that Fatkins diet.'

'Fatkins? Yer mean Atkins yer daft 'apporth!' berated a half-cut Linda.

'Tek nee notice pet,' said Stuart. 'He's dyslexic.'

'I was tekking the rise, yer divvy,' carped Roy.

'Oh . . . I get it it now,' giggled an enlightened Linda.

'Hallelujah,' muttered Janet.

'Fatkins instead of Atkins because yer were being rude about her weight.'

'By, yer on good form today our lass.'

'What does dyslexic mean?' asked Billy, at the risk of derision from the usual quarter. He was surprised when none emerged.

Janet explained, 'Basically it's a disorder characterised by difficulty in reading, writing and spelling. It's just another word for someone who's thick. Don't quote me though. I'm putting a facetious spin on it cos I feel that way out today. Another example of modern gobbledygook is when they say an insufferable kid has ADD.'

'Yer've lost me. What does that stand for?'

'Attention deficit disorder.'

'I'm still nee wiser,' conceded Billy.

'It's another stupid diagnosis allowing obnoxious, undisciplined kids to act like spoilt brats. Everything's an illness these days. Nobody takes responsibility anymore. In reality, the little shits are in need of a good hiding. They say it worked in the past. This country's too full of them wishy-washy liberal types. Everything's got to be PC.'

'Hey, lighten-up girl,' advised Alistair. 'You're getting a bit philosophical on us love.'

'I'm just educating your hillbilly relatives,' she teased, winking at Billy who went on to thank her for the information anyway.

'Atkins . . . ' deliberated Roy as if in a state of time delay the past few minutes. 'The old boys 'ave been on that diet all their lives an' look at the state of them! Not exactly a shining endorsement for it, are they?'

'Aye, that's true,' nodded Stuart in agreement.

'Ah, but they're still alive though,' pointed out Billy.

'Whey, that's debatable,' sneered Roy.

'You are awful,' chuckled Linda. 'I'll 'ave to meet these old boys sometime.'

'That's easily remedied bonny lass cos they're all in there scoffing their faces with the Atkins diet,' stated Roy, indicating towards the luncheon room.

'Yorkshire pudding and roast beef actually,' corrected Billy.

'Well, I'll not intrude on their meal,' I'm too well mannered for that,' said Linda, her face contorted in a snob-like manner.

'As if,' derided Janet. 'You're common as muck.'

'At least I'm not Lady Muck.'

'No bickering you two. Hard as it is for you both,' berated Alistair.

Roy had decided now was time to unveil some of his side splitting jokes onto the lucky gathering.

'Listen up peeps, I's ganna tell a few brilliant jokes,' he announced.

'Oh no,' groaned Billy, putting his head in his hands.

'Let the hilarity begin without further ado.'

'A sigh of resignation reverberated through what was formerly a happy group. Frozen, like rabbits caught in the headlights.

'Did you hear aboot the Siamese twins who went holidaying in Spain every year so the other one could drive?'

'Dear me,' uttered Janet.

'Listen, there's more.'

'Get on with it then Jimmy Cricket,' urged Billy.

Roy obliged, 'Did you here aboot the dyslexic, agnostic insomniac? He lay awake all night wondering if there really was a Dog.' Roy looked around for any reactions. 'Too clever for yer that one?' he questioned.

'No, I got it,' said Janet, while the others just looked bemused, hoping Roy would get on to the next joke sharpish.

'My wife told me I was nosey. Well, she didn't tell me - I read it in her diary.'

A few chuckles ensued.

'Ar could tell when we crossed into Yorkshire this morning - The motorway was cobbled.'

'Watch it lad,' said Linda, but smiling all the same.

'Ower local ice-cream man was found dead yesterday. He was found with nuts and chocolate and raspberry sauce on his head. The police say he'd topped himself.'

The last gag bringing much merriment, Roy was encouraged to carry on.

'During the last war my granda wouldn't gan in the air raid shelter when the siren went. He said 'If a bomb's got your name on it, there's nowt yer can do." He survived. Unfortunately his next door neighbours, Mr an' Mrs Doodlebug didn't.'

Mixed reactions on the old laugh-o-meter - a few of them not knowing what a doodlebug was.

'Last week I was walking home an' decided to tek a short cut ower the railway line when I saw this naked bird tied to the track. I told me mate that I back scuttled her, went down on her an' gave her a tit wank. He said, "Did she give yer a blow job?" Ar told him I didn't cos I couldn't find her head.'

Alistair spluttered on his beer. Even for Roy, this was crude. This girls looked at each other incredulously then burst into laughter, while Billy and Stuart cringed, having heard the joke before.

'That's really sick,' laughed Janet. 'Funny, but sick.'

'That's an understatement,' added Linda with tears in her eyes.

'Thank God,' muttered Billy to Stuart. 'Here comes Don in the nick of time. Like a bald knight in shining armour.'

'Hello everybody. All enjoying yer sens are yer?' he greeted.

'Hey up, it's uncle Fester! Janet, Linda, this is Don, one of ower geriatric contingent,' introduced Roy in his own irreverent manner. 'Yer wouln't believe it but this time last year he had a full head of healthy brown hair.'

'What happened to it?' asked Janet, hoping she hadn't put her foot in it, wondering if he'd suffered cancer and losing his hair through treatment.

'Whey, yer nar that shampoo, Wash an' Gan?'

'Yes.'

'Well, Don washed his hair in it . . . an' it went!' chortled Roy.

'Tek nee notice of him bonny lasses,' said Don. 'If ar had a pund fer every time he told that joke aboot me, ar'd be a rich man.'

'Doesn't Don remind yer of someone?' asked Roy.

'Can't say he does,' pondered Janet.

'Me neither,' said Linda.

'Don't yer remember that little bald bloke Benny Hill used to slap around the heed all the time?'

'Oh, I know who you mean,' recalled Linda. 'No offence Don.'

'None tekken pet. It's all watter off a duck's back concerning bugger lugs.'

'He's a canny singer mind is Don, ar'll give him that,' praised Roy.

'Where's the catch?'

'No catch Don. Credit where credit's due. You wouldn't believe the amount of bloomers he gets thrown at him singing at the Phoenix over 80s night.'

'He doesn't,' doubted Linda.

'It's true - honest. Have yer heard of Long John Baldry, a singer from the 60s?'

'No.'

'Never mind. This is Short Don Baldy - the tribute act.'

'All that to get a pathetic bald gag in?'

'Please yer sen.'

'Anyway, listen-up boys and girls,' said Don. 'The reason I'm out here - apart from having the pleasure of meeting you two charming young ladies of course . . . '

'Stop perving you old git. Someone pass me the sick bucket,' ridiculed Roy.

Don ignored him. 'As I was saying, I was asked by our generous landlord John Craig, to offer everybody a drink, care of his wallet - not mine I hasten to add!'

'As if! Well why didn't yer say man? said Roy, knocking back the remainder of his pint. 'Come on, stop sniffing round the lasses an' ar'll give yer a hand wi' the ale. Same again is it girls?'

'No thanks Roy, I think our lass has had enough for one day. Besides, we're meeting Steve shortly and we've a bit more shopping to do.'

'Spoilsport,' grumbled Linda. 'But as it happens, bossy boots, I know I've had enough anyway.'

Entering the bar with Roy, Don was relieved to see that the punters had thinned out a bit. Roy headed for the gents leaving Don at the bar to order the drinks.

'Are you gonna nip in the luncheon room Janet an' see me grandad before you go?' asked Alistair.

'Not now, if it's all the same to you. I'll wait until I come up to Stanhope show in September. I can meet all your relations then.'

'Yeah, whatever suits you love,' agreed Alistair, immediately understanding that it would be a little uncomfortable and embarrassing for Janet to walk into a room full of high-spirited strangers, no matter how genial they may be.

Don and Roy were soon back with the drinks, Roy chomping at the bit to get his mouth back into gear.

'I'm not kidding but I was in the gents just now an' standing next to me 'aving a piss was this huge darkie. Honest to God, his bell end was aboot half an inch from the moth-balls at the bottom of the trough. His dick was as thick as a poitician's wallet. It was nearly as big as mine - I kid ye not! Though in all modesty, my tip did brush against the old moth-balls.'

'Roy's classic monologues must have the intellectual wordsmiths of yesteryear turning in their graves,' stated Don.

'I bet you can't wait to go up north our lass,' remarked Linda.

'You'll come back so refined and full of knowledge - not!'

'Don't you worry Linda, we'll keep as far away from our Roy as possible,' Alistair assured her.

'Like hell yer will!' contradicted Roy, turning to Janet.

'Divent you be fretting pet. I'll keep yer entertained and amused, nee problem.'

'That's very thoughtful of you Roy. I'm honoured,' said a disingenuous Janet.

'Think nowt of it bonny lass. I'm reknown fer my hospitality, and being a Weardale socialite, I get invited to all the 'A' list gatherings. It gans wi'out saying, you're welcome to come along any time, just say the word. If yer must, yer can bring along Yorky now an' again.'

'Weardale socialite,' sneered Alistair. 'Weadale bag o' shite more like. 'A ' list gatherings my arse . . . They've only just started line dancing up there. It's held in the town hall. That's the nearest you'll get a night club. Mind you, fair do's an' credit where credit's due - they are trying to modernise and embrace the 20th century.'

'Ar think you mean the 21st century there,' corrected Roy.

'No, I mean the 20th. They've only just got the drinking licence extended to 9.30 on a Saturday night. Believe me, that's progress for Stanhope.'

Roy gave Alistair the finger before lighting up a cigarette, while Don said farewell to the girls and rejoined the dining party inside the pub.

'Look at that idiot ganning in there!' remarked Billy.

'Where?' asked Stuart turning round.

'Yer've just missed him.'

'Who was it like? Someone famous?'

'Nar, but someone who wishes they were. It were one o' them sad David beckham look-a-likes. They must be that insecure, they canna get a life of their own,' deplored Billy.

'Aye, yer reet. Everybody wants to be somebody else, tragic bastards. Excuse my language,' apologised Stuart with a chuckle.

'Divent knock it, yer set o' puffs. Having more than a few Roy Osborne look-i-likies throughout the land, ar tek it as a compliment,' he swaggered.

'Arraway an' shite yer deluded prig. Who in their reet mind wants to walk aboot looking like the back end of a bus?'

'Sez he that stinks o' sour milk all the time. Ar'll tek nee lectures from ye Ernie.'

'Ernie?' puzzled Billy.

'Aye - he drove the fastest milk cart in the west. That Benny Hill song, remember?'

'Oh, aye. What a crap song that was.'

'Like that Pop Idol rubbish - ar've seen better singers down the pub,' derided Stuart.

'Yer reet there,' endorsed Billy.

'I nar I am. If that show's got any redeeming features, it's that judge Simon Cowell - the man in black wi' his trousers up to his armpits. He doesn't sit on the fence. Tells 'em to their face, "That was a load of shite - Next!" He's ace.'

'Aye, he's the only good thing in the show,' said Billy in agreement. 'Them other three muppets talk shite. Pete Waterman, "Not fer me kid" What's he nar? A tone deaf old age pensioner! An' she nars bugger all aboot singing an' all - that blonde minger judge, always drooling ower the young ens. Gans fer the one wi' the most socks tucked down his calvins. "I think you were great this week", her knickers getting wetter an' wetter. What they call that other judge?'

'Foxy,' obliged Roy.

'Aye, that's him - Foxy. Who named him that? He's fattest fox ar've ever seen. Dogs'd catch him easy. He'd never get down the hole to escape! What's his mantra . . . "I thought you were a tad shite this week, like last week an' the week afore that" A pile o' crap - all of it!'

'Yer not wrong Billy,' said Roy. 'That Will Young only won by kidding on he was a fudge pusher . . . ganning fer the pink vote. It worked mind. Against all odds he beat that favourite, Gareth Gates. He can sing a bit - but he canna talk. People said it was a fix. Folks were voting but couldn't get through. Mind yer, what do they expect phoning from Bradford, it's probably only got one phone line. Bradford . . . the arsehole of Leeds, as it's more commonly known.'

'Don't you be knocking Bradford,' protested Linda.

'He's winding you up,' Alistair informed her.

'Gareth Gates might 'ave come second but he still made it to the top.'

'Oh aye, yer reet there bonny lass,' said Roy patronisingly. 'He got to number one wi' that old Who classic.'

'I don't remember him singing a Who song.'

'Yer divent? An' you, a local lass? It was that, Talking about my g-g-g-generation.'

'You're a cruel sod!' derided Linda.

'Whey, it's reet. He made a load o' brass advertising fer that margarine company an' all.'

'I'm not listening,' said Linda covering her ears with her hands.

'What margarine?' asked Janet.

'Yer can't tell Stork from stutter,' chortled Roy.

'You're a sick man.'

'Whey yer divent need to pity the lad Janet,' insisted Roy. 'He managed to give that big bapped bird one - Jordan. Whey, he couldn't say "no".'

'Say nowt love, you'll only encourage him,' Alistair advised Janet.

'Ar just tell it how it is. Nowt wrong wi' that Yorky boy.'

Janet looked at her watch. 'Time we made tracks.'

'Aw, do yer 'ave to gan?' pleaded Roy. 'Hang aboot wi' us, mek a day of it. Yer can show us the sights an' what 'ave yer.'

'Thanks but no thanks. Maybe another time.'

'Linda.'

'Yes Roy?'

'Do you fancy tagging along with us fer the rest o' the day?'

'I don't think so.'

'Ha way, live a little. Kick that loser boyfriend o' yours into touch an' trip the light fantastic wi' the Weardale stud.'

'Oh, alright, go on then.'

'Honest Linda?'

'Don't be stupid man! I'm winding *you* up now.'

'Whey it's your loss love. There's lasses'd kill to gan oot wi' me.

154

Yer divent nar what yer missing.'

'Go with them then,' suggested Linda.

'Divent worry bonny lass. By the end of tonight, ar'll 'ave a wench on each arm. An' if they're lucky, ar might tek 'em back to hedonistic Stanhope. There's a few spare seats aboard the lurve bus.'

'Hedonistic Stanhope? The village is full of luddites,' mocked Alistair. 'If it wasn't for DVDs an' videos, they'd have no entertainment at all. Nearest cinema to Stanhope is twenty miles away.'

'What the hec are luddites?' asked Roy.

Alistair went on to explain. 'The Luddites were a group of artisans who in the early 19th century systematically destroyed machinery - especially in the textile industry. This was because they feared that the increase in automation not only threatened job security, but also resulted in the production of shoddier goods. Or singularly, Luddite was anyone who opposed new technology or industrial change. Said to be named after Ned Lud or Ludd, who, far from being the leader of the group, as popularity believed, was someone who had attacked hosiery maufacturing equipment in an insane frenzy some thirty years earlier.'

Roy was not impressed with what he perceived as Alistair showing off in front of the girls. 'I bet you've been rehearsing that useless, inane piece of information fer months, yer Yorkshire ponce,' he said with derision.

'No he hasn't,' protested Janet.

'Give ower, he's a boring swot,' insisted Roy.

'Just because he's a walking encyclopaedia, it doesn't follow that he's boring as well. On the contrary, Alistair's knowledgeable mind is only a small part of his magnetism.'

'So, what's a good night in fer ye two? Discussing the works of William Shakespeare ower a cup of cocoa? Or fretting ower underlying inflation mebbe? Lighten up. Divent tek life so serious. Yer'll never get out alive. Worrying's like a rocking chair - It gets yer nowhere.'

'Who's being the philosopher now?' derided Janet.

The irony of his little monologue was not lost on Roy. On the contrary, it was intentional.

'Roy's idea of culture is a million miles from yours Janet,' stated Billy.

'What's his idea then?'

'Sophistication in Roy's world is dropping his kecks an' squatting his bare arse cheeks into newly laid concrete an' leaving his mark for all to see. That's his equivalent of an American star leaving their handprint on that Hollywood pavement - or sidewalk, as the yanks like to call it. Aye . . . Roy's buttock artistry, north east region, is second only to The Angel of the North.'

'Whey, it's modern art Billy boy,' insisted Roy.

'Modern arse, more like.'

'Whey, at least ar'll 'ave left a legacy fer future art lovers to view.'

'Yer joking man! Ower cowboy concreting'll 'ave crumbled well afore you've kicked the bucket.'

'That's true,' conceded Roy, smiling. 'But I'm working on an invention of my own.'

'What invention?' asked Billy.'

'Skid-mark concrete. It's a future phenom . . . phenormarvel.'

'Phenomenon.'

'Aye, that an' all.'

'As interesting as this conversation is, we must love you and leave you now,' said Janet picking up several carrier bags, Linda picking up the remainder.

Alistair kissed Janet, promising to phone her the following day.

'Bye everyone. It's been nice meeting you all,' said Linda.

'You too pet,' said Stuart and Billy.

'I'll probably see you all when I come up for Stanhope Show!' called Janet as they set off down the yard.

'Aye, see yer! shouted Roy. 'Bugger off back to t'mill me old flowers! An' divent be worrying aboot Alistair's best man, come the wedding, cos it'll be an honour. Just leave the job in my capable hands!'

'Thanks Roy! I'll sleep better tonight knowing that!' grinned Janet.

A final wave and the sisters disappeared amongst the Briggate crowds.

'Did I mention marriage our lass?' asked Janet.

'Not to my knowledge.'

'I thought not.'

'Cheer up Alistair lad,' said Roy. 'It's only a fortnight afore yer see yer future spouse agen. Unless she hitches up wi' someone else meantime like.'

'No way,' responded Alistair.

'Whey, in the interim like, ar'll gladly fix you up wi' one of my superfluous to requirement young ladies - nee bother.'

'That's very considerate of you Royston - I appreciate the gesture. Thanks, but no thanks. I have every intention of returning home without contracting any sort of sexually transmitted disease. No offence like.'

'No offence? Yer cheeky pillock! Ar'll 'ave you nar, all my ladies are of the highest order. Top totty. Exclusively conserved on behalf of the Weardale stud. All patiently waiting by their mobiles until I beckon them forth fer a good rogering. Usually by which time they're foaming at the mouth like rabid dogs in anticipation of reaching the promised land - the Garden of Eden, because their orgasm is of biblical proportions.'

'Do you practice safe sex Roy?' asked Alistair nonchalantly, just going through the motions.

'Practice?' exclaimed Roy. 'There's nee practice when it comes to sex with the master. It's expertise sex bonny lad.'

'You know what I mean - Do you use condoms?'

'Most of the time I do.'

'Why not all the time? Especially in todays climes regards unprotected sex.'

'It depends on whether the extra large condom machine runs out in the Phoenix. John had it especially installed for me, but his stock tekking skills leave summat to be desired. Hence, on the odd occasion I do ride bareback. But ar can honestly say ar've never had so much as an itchy scrotum - touch wood. Mind you, what's life wi'out an element of risk bonny lad? As long as yer divent get ower paranoid, yer'll enjoy a canny sex life. Worrying's fer losers man. Did yer nar I had a nickname amongst the elite Weardale lasses?'

'An' what's that then - Bighead?'

'No, clever dick.'

'Clever dick! How ground-breaking!'

'Stop messing, yer skinny ponce. I am affectionately referred to as rigor mortis.'

'Go on then, Linford Christie, I'll indulge you - why rigor mortis?'

'He always falls asleep on the job, that's why,' chipped in Stuart.

'Aye, he's usually comatosed with ale,' added Billy.

'Who rattled your cages?' sniped Roy. 'I'm known as rigor mortis because I can keep an erection all neet long. Cock o' the north is another monicker I get tagged wi'. All very flattering ar must admit, but it fair embarrasses me at times.'

'As if. Pull the other one,' mocked Stuart. 'There's more chance of Phoney Blair passing a lie detector test than you getting embarrassed.'

'It's true man. I may have it all, but ar like to think I keep a modicum of humility tucked to one side.'

'Now, there's two words I thought I would never hear in the same sentence.'

'What's that Alistair?' asked Billy.

'Roy and humility.'

'Aye, well . . . Sometimes Yorky, you have to look beyond the facade,' said Roy, in all false modesty.

'Well, you'd have to look long and hard to see through your facade. You've got more front than Blackpool. Yer a thick-skinned bugger if nothing else.'

'Arraway an' shite man.'

'I'm nipping fer a slash,' declared Stuart. 'Anyone want a drink while I'm in there?'

'Mek sure yer wash yer hands after shekking that hamster dick,' goaded Roy.

'Bollocks, yer big gob shite!' retorted Stuart.

'Leave the drinks fer now Stewpot,' suggested Billy. 'We'll see yer inside. Time's knocking on, so we'll see what the rest of the rabble 'ave planned first.'

'Aye, reet yer are.' Stuart headed for the gents reflecting as he did, how much more frequently he seemed to empty his bladder compared to drinking in the Phoenix. Must be the change in beer, he convinced himself. That, or the Yorkshire water.

'Divent look now chaps, but there's three of Ken Dodd's Diddymen heading this way,' Roy informed them. 'Either that or there's a dwarf throwing contest ganning on or mebbe a Ronnie Corbett convention's in towm.'

'Don't be taking the piss an' showing us up,' warned Alistair in no uncertain terms. 'They can't help being vertically challenged.'

'Vertically challenged my arse. They're dwarfs man. Stop being so PC. Besides, I'm just naturally curious towards 'em. It's alright fer you, but we never see dwarfs in Stanhope. They're as rare as a village Post Office. Hi ho, hi ho, it's off to work we go,' sang Roy.

'Oh no,' cringed Alistair.

'Shut it Roy man,' admonished Billy.

'Stop fretting. Are yer alreet little fellows?' said Roy greeting the dwarfs. 'Where's Snow White then?'

'Back in my waterside apartment big fellow,' came the jovial reply, seemingly not in the least offended by Roy's comments. After all, it wasn't as if they hadn't heard it all before.

'Your speel's not very original son,' said another of the dwarfs, again without the hint of malice.

'Aye, ar suppose yer've heard it all afore,' conceded Roy. 'Still, if yer need a hand wi' Snow White, yer nar where I am.'

'Will do. But don't hold yer breath lad.'

'Are yer in a rush? Can I get you a drink? Three halves mebbe?'

'No thanks,' they declined in unison.'

'Something to eat then? A piece of shortbread?'

'You're getting worse young 'en. Don't give up the day job,' advised the first dwarf.

Wishing the lads a good day on the town they continued down the passage onto Briggate.

'Well, they were nice enough,' remarked Billy. 'They didn't get piqued at your baiting Roy. One of 'em could easily 'ave given you a head-butt in the bollocks. Justifiably as well. Ar divent nar what they do fer a living but you could tell they were professional men. Cool an' totally unfazed.'

'They're not from outer space yer know. As I said before, they're just normal people but vertically challenged,' Alistair reminded them. 'You definitely must get out more.'

'Come off yer high horse Yorky. Me an' Billy will be getting out a lot more. When we've handed in ower notice next week, that's us away. The world's our lobster.'

'Oyster Roy.'

'No thanks, they're too slimy.'

'Anyway, come off it.' Alistair wasn't having any of this "handing in their notice" rubbish.

'Come off what?' questioned Roy.

'All this crap about packing in your jobs! You two'll be in Stanhope for the rest of your lives. Yer'll still be propping up the bar in the Phoenix when you're seventy. Talking the same old bollocks as the old boys do now.'

'If I end up propping up the Phoenix bar, it'll be as the owner. And ar'll have a whole chain of pubs an' all - not just one like idle John,' insisted Roy.

'In your dreams,' sneered Alistair.

'We'll see.'

The lads went inside the bustling, and somewhat boisterous Whitelocks.

'God, yer can't breathe in here,' complained Alistair, emitting an exaggerated cough.

'That's cos yer divent smoke,' pointed out Billy.

'Aye, we're used to it,' added Roy.

Primed with an abundance of alcohol, the clientele were in high spirits. Stuart, having been to the gents, had already joined the ebullient eating party in the luncheon room. Without exception, they each had a glass of brandy in one hand and a King Edward's cigar in the other - compliments again of their generous and favourite (for today anyway) landlord. All were chatting away ten to the dozen, clearly relaxed and thoroughly enjoying themselves.

'Hold up lads,' heralded Roy stopping in his tracks, arms outstretched, 'We're in the wrong room. We've walked into the rehearsal room of The Sopranos. Have yer ever seen owt like it in your life? A gathering of the Weardale Godfathers!' he laughed.

'Divent knock it bonny lad,' said Frank.

'He's just jealous man,' said old Tom.

'Huh! Listen to him. That cigar's fatter than you Tom. It looks like yer smoking a log from where I'm standing,' mocked Roy. 'It was only a couple of hours ago yer were at death's door - sat puffing an' panting outside the market. Ar tek it yer feeling better then?'

'Oh aye, much better young en. It's amazing.'

'What is?'

'The healing power of some free booze an' grub,' grinned Tom cheekily.

'I bet.'

'Did you all enjoy the meal then?' asked Alistair.

'Oh aye, canny grub an' no mistake,' 'Spot on,' and 'Real Yorkshire fare at its best,' were just a few of the favourable comments.

A waiter placed the bill on the table.

'Here you are minehost, this is yours I believe,' said Ronnie, passing the bill to John.

John put on his reading glasses, 'One hundred an' twelve quid all inclusive. Cheap at half the price,' he proclaimed.

'Whey, it's much appreciated,' said Fred with gratitude.

'Aye, thanks John,' added Alf.

'Think nothing of it gentlemen. Besides, I'll get it all back in my till.'

'How d'yer mek that out?' asked Fred.

'Well, come November, or whenever it is yer get yer two hundred quid fuel allowance - yer'll spend it in the Phoenix, which when yer think, is only proper seeing as yer keep yer sens warm in my pub every lunchtime an' night.'

'Aye, yer don't find 'em complaining aboot the government when that cheque drops in their lap do yer?' skitted Don, out of the blue.'

'Fair do's to the government on that score Don,' conceded Fred.

'Divent get me wrong. It's very welcome,' added Alf.

161

'Aye, the tories wouldn't 'ave awarded us a lump sum,' said Tom. 'If only the weekly pension was significantly raised instead of being based against the yearly rate of inflation. Always peanuts.'

'Ar'll second that Tom lad,' said Fred in agreement.

Roy challenged John, 'What happened to ower brandy then?'

'To be honest with yer, ar thought it was too potent a drink fer you young ens to handle,' teased John.

'Whey, yer nar what thought did,' sneered Roy, referring to an old country saying.

'What did thought do?' asked Alistair with curiosity.

Roy obliged, 'Thought thought he'd shit him sen. When he looked, he had. Don't ask - it's gobbledygook to me an' all.'

In fact, no one gathered there knew the origins of the inane words or their meaning and to this day it remains ambiguous and rarely used of late.

'John's reet though son. Brandy's far too strong fer the likes of ye young apprentice boozers,' taunted old Tom.

'You wanna watch what you say, you old timers. Any more lip an' ar'll boycott your rapidly impending funerals,' threatened the acerbic Roy.

'Whey we'll not lose any sleep ower that laddie,' Tom assured him.

John removed his wallet from his inside jacket pocket. Taking out a ten pound note, he handed it to Roy. 'There's a tenner. Owt to shut you up. Get yer sen an' the lads a short each. An' while yer at the bar, yer can pay my bill please.' He counted out a hundred and fifteen pounds onto the table. 'The bill's a hundred and twelve quid. Tell the waiter to keep the change will yer?'

'Bloody hell! The last of the big spenders. He'll be booking him sen a fortneets holiday in the Bahamas tomorrow.'

'Just pay the bill gobby.'

'Yes sir,' genuflected Roy before turning to the lads and querying their favoured short.

'Three rums an' a Baileys fer the nancy boy,' concluded Roy with a sneer.

'There's nowt wrong wi' that,' protested Alistair. 'I'm not

162

drinking rum just to please you. I like the odd Baileys, so I'll have a Baileys, thank you very much.'

'Alreet, keep yer hair on Alison,' goaded Roy. 'D'yer want a cherry an' a little umbrella with it?'

'No. Baileys on its own'll do.'

Placing the tray of drinks on the table and sitting next to Stuart, Roy sought John's attention. 'The waiter told me to send you his utmost thanks for your generous tip landlord. Apparently he's tekking a years sabbatical on it. I'm sure he mentioned summat aboot ganning on a world tour.'

'Yer a sarcastic sod,' sighed John. 'I've a good mind . . . '

'That's a matter of opinion, mocked Roy.'

'Let me finish pillock face. As I was saying - I've a good mind to tek that rum off you, fer all yer cheek.'

'Ar divent nar aboot sarcastic . . . ' contradicted Stuart, 'Well, yeah, ar suppose he is that . . . but he's a sadistic piece of work.'

'How d'yer mean?' asked old Tom.

'Whey, ar divent like being a snitch like.'

'Since when?' skitted Roy.

'Go on Stuart,' encouraged John.

'Alright. As a kid, Roy used to superglue breadcrumbs to the windowsill, an' then watch the birds getting a hernia, trying to peck them off.'

'You're a sick person Roy Osborne - no mistekking,' derided John.

'Divent believe a word of it - I'm beyond reproach,' insisted Roy.

'It's all true,' stressed Stuart.

'If you say it's true, that's good enough for me,' taunted John.

'It's all porkies,' protested Roy. 'He's a bigger liar than that bent Major twat that tried hoodwinking "Who wants to be a millionaire" - whey, him an' that ugly wife of his an' a fat ponce wi' TB o' the lungs sat in the front row of the audience, coughing in all the reet places. Ar wouldn't mind so much, but the corrupt bastards kept popping up on every other TV programme denying it all! The bare-faced cheek of some folks - it's unbelievable,' he smirked.

'Whey, it's only the sort of scam you'd come up wi' Roy,'

163

pointed out Stuart.

'Maybe,' admitted Roy. 'But then, ar wouldn't get caught like that set o' knob-head amateurs.'

Deep in conversation with a local man, Arthur hadn't noticed the lads. He was having an in depth discussion about football - Leeds United being the main issue. Getting on like a house on fire, you'd think they'd known each other all their lives.

Alistair managed to grab his grandfather's attention. 'I've just remembered you wanted a Leeds United book an' video from Borders. I'm sorry grandad, but they'll be closed now.'

'Not to worry Alistair, you can get them for me when yer get back from Stanhope. Ar'll give yer the money an' yer can post 'em on to me. Eeh, ar can't believe how fast the time's gone. By the way, this gentlemen ar've been talking to is Albert Grimshaw,' said Arthur introducing his companion.

'A southerner eh?' muttered Roy.

'He's a semi professional golfer an' lives in Adel. That's a posh part of Leeds by the way,' added Arthur. 'They even get out o' the bath fer a pee in Adel,' he chuckled.

'Roy doesn't even get out o' the bath fer a shite,' muttered Stuart.

Arthur then went on to introduce the lads individually to his new found friend.

Roy picked up one of the daily tabloids from the untidy pile in the middle of the table.

Alf was ficking through one of the plethora of magazines that accompanied the Saturday papers which only amounted to about a third of what was attached to the Sunday papers. Many a person had ended up with a hernia caused by the sheer volume of magazines and scratch cards (every one a winner) that were tucked between the pages of their chosen newspaper.

Pausing and shaking his head from time to time, everyone knew Alf was building up to a negative comment.

'Eeh . . . ar divent nar,' he tutted.

'What divent yer nar,' asked Frank.

'Whey, these advertisers. They must think we've just dropped off a Christmas tree.'

'How come Alfred?'

'Tek this advert fer personal insurance - "Aged between 50 and 80 . . . " '

'That's ye excluded then,' goaded Roy.

'Shut it you! As I was trying to convey . . . ' Alf gave Roy a dirty look. ' "Aged between 50 and 80? For as little as eight pound a month we will cover your health insurance needs. No medical required. No conmen salesmen will call on you. Sign up within ten days and receive a complimentary prestigious gold plated biro - ar mean Parker Pen." What a load of dog's bollocks!'

'Ar nar exactly what you mean Alfred,' nodded Tom in agreement. 'It's the same every time yer switch on yer telly. There's allus some company or other trying to flog you an assortment of health policies or loans. They flash some small print at the bottom of the screen at the end of the advert that lasts aboot a milli-second. You'd 'ave to video it an' put it on pause an' use a telescope to read all the subject to status an' get out clauses.'

'Subject to Status?' skitted Roy. 'That's ye oldies knackered fer starters. Yer've nee chance. Full-time piss artists won't cut much ice with 'em.'

'Smart alec,' sneered Alf.

As happened only on rare occasions, Fred's thoughts had been ignited by the conversation and he added his two pennorth. 'Divent talk to me aboot TV advertising. I've had it up to here,' he demonstrated, bringing up the back of his hand underneath his chin. 'That Christopher Timothy.'

'Who?' asked Billy.

'Christopher Timothy - that actor that played the vet in that telly series years ago . . . I'm damned if ar can remember the name of it . . . '

'All Creatures great and small,' obliged Frank.'

'Aye, that's it. Cheers Frank. Anyway, back to my story. Everytime it was on, this Timothy fellow seemed to have his arm stuck up a cow's arse.'

'Urgh, the dirty pervert. He'd be arrested fer that nowadays,' cringed the disingenuous Roy.

'He was usually aiding the extraction of a newborn calf, yer big divvy,' derided Fred. 'Yer've put me off me stride now. Where was I?' he contemplated, rubbing his forehead.

'Christopher Timothy,' prompted Ronnie.

'Aye, that's it. He's never off the box - telling you to invest in that Cornhill Direct as quickly as possible cos yer probably ganna drop dead any second now an' it'd be nice to leave some brass fer yer loved ones.'

'That dun't apply to you Fred,' baited Roy.

'How d'yer mek that out?'

'Because you 'aven't got any loved ones.'

'Very droll - yer shite-hawk.'

Not yet finished his wind up, Roy carried on, 'Eight pund a month yer say Alf?'

'Aye, ar did.'

'Yer can buy two pints o' lager in the Phoenix fer eight pund.'

'Hey, watch it sonny,' warned John with little conviction as he leafed through the Express. 'It says here that this so-called New Labour party are going to introduce tuition fees for English students,' he stated.

'Will that be the same political party that said they wouldn't be introducing tuition fees in their last manifesto?' queried Frank.

'The very same,' confirmed John.

'They've got to get the money fer further education from somewhere,' said Don in Labour's defence.

'Why divent they use the money - probably billions - that's spent on bombing innocent Iraqi citizens in an illegal war?' confronted John.

Don's silence spoke volumes.

John continued his tirade. 'They don't have tuition fees in Scotland and Wales. What really gets my back up is that the jocks an' taffys can vote on policies affecting England, whilst English politicians are not allowed to vote on their policies. What a fucking sham!'

'Now, now John, settle down. No politics when we're imbibing- remember?' Ronnie pointed out.

'Aye, yer right. Subject closed.'

Roy felt that one of his infamous jokes was well overdue. Professing to quote from a page of his newspaper, 'Do yer nar, they reckon millions of people every year catch Aids from mosquitos? Well I'm sorry, but anyone who goes around fucking mosquitos' deserve all they get.'

Laughs resounded all around the table and Roy lapped it up. His only reservation was what his grandad's response would be to the bad language. He needn't have worried. A quick glance in his direction saw Arthur and his new found pal laughing as much as the next man. Roy was chuffed with himself.

'Ar divent nar aboot you Billy, but ar fancy trying another wattering hole,' said Stuart.

'Aye, me an' all.' Billy nudged Roy.

'Yes, what can ar do yer for?'

'Me an' Stew fancy a bit of a toby round. What yer think?'

'Sounds good to me, bonny lad. Let's see what the rest of this rabble's deeing. 'Grandad!' shouted Roy.

'Yes son?'

'Me an' the lads are thinking of mekking a move to another boozer. Are yer coming with us or staying put?'

Arthur consulted the rowdy bunch of their immediate plans. After a few moments he looked up. 'Okay lads, you get off an' enjoy yer sens. We'll meet up with yer later in a pub on the Headrow - the Vine - say aboot nine o'clockish. Alistair nars where it is.' Arthur was enjoying himself far too much to be moving on just yet. Like the rest of the Weardale clan, he was having a ball.

Saying their farewells and confirming the time and place of their rendezvous, the younger lads set off down Turks Head Yard towards Briggate. They passed a middle-aged man relieving himself in the narrow alleyway on the opposite wall to the Whitelocks.

'Are yer al . . . reet lads?' he slurred, wobbling unsteadily on his feet, one hand against the wall for balance and spraying his feet with urine in the process.

'Aye, champion mate,' replied Roy. 'And you?'

'Reet as rain lad. Reet as - hic! - fucking rain. Oh the old town, hic, looked the same, as he stepped down - hic - from the train. And there to meet me - hic - was my mama and papa . . . ' he sang accompanied by a volley of farts.

'One o' them farts must 'ave been a wet one, ar'll put money on it,' chuckled Roy, making sure he was out of earshot. 'An' ar bet he catches his foreskin in his zipper an' all. Poor drunken bastard. One day, these Yorkshire bumpkins'll be toilet trained.'

'Huh! Listen to pot calling kettle black,' sniped Billy.

'Ar haven't got the foggiest what yer on aboot,' carped Roy.

'Whey, you piss up against the fire station wall most neets on the way home from the Phoenix.'

'Divent exaggerate man! I may have emptied my bladder in an extreme emergency, granted.'

'Bollocks!'

'Roy was adamant. 'It's true. Besides, you've pissed again the fire station an' all, yer hypocrite.'

'Yeah okay, I admit it. But very, very rarely. Mebbe once in a blue moon when ar've been absolutely blotto.'

'Give ower, yer'll tell us owt man.'

'Stop arguing yer pair o' girls,' berated Stuart. 'Where we ganning Alistair? Ar've got the taste fer it,' he said rubbing his hands together. 'This is your home territory.'

'Well, I live in Leeds but I don't often drink in the central pubs,' pondered Alistair.

'It canna be that hard Yorky. There's dozens of pubs to gan at,' said Roy.

'Alright Geordie, don't be so impatient. There's the Ship just up there,' suggested Alistair.

'Say nee more. That'll dee bonny lad,' said Roy slapping Alistair on the back. 'It's not as busy as ar though it'd be fer a Saturday neet,' he commented, looking up and down Briggate.

'Give it time Roy, it's early. The night's still young. Folks get primed wi' booze at home before they come to town pubbing an' clubbing. It's a lot cheaper.'

'Aye, yer canna blame 'em like.'

Following Alistair, they turned left up a narrow passageway. A few steps up it brought them to the Ship Inn.

Chapter 9

The pub was about half full, consisting of mainly younger customers. Males out numbering the females.

'Your shout Alistair lad,' prompted Stuart.

'Is it? Four pints of lager then.'

They made their way to the bar with relative ease and were served quickly. Finding a corner table, they sat themselves down. Seated nearby were three attractive, nicely dressed young ladies who appeared to be be thoroughly enjoying themselves, laughing and chatting away.

Billy thought he'd introduce himself and the others sharpish before the most undiplomatic person on earth - namely Roy - got in there first and scared them off.

'You're definitely mekking the most of your neet out ladies,' said Billy with no lack of confidence.

'Too true we are,' came the reply. 'If you can't enjoy a Saturday night out in Leeds you never will.'

Billy introduced himself and the lads before asking the girls their names.

'I'm Laura, the best looking and the oldest.'

'That's a matter of opinion.'

'*That* was my sister Katy, and this is Elisa.'

'Pleased to meet you,' greeted the lads.

'If yer divent mind me saying, yer the best looking Yorkshire lasses ar've seen today,' said Roy.

'Thanks for the compliment. Nice of you to say so,' said Katy.

'My pleasure.'

Alistair squirmed, thinking to himself, if only they knew the real Roy.

'Are you from Leeds or visiting?' asked Elisa.

'We're on a day trip pet,' explained Stuart. 'We gan back at ten o'clock - worse luck,' he sighed.

'With that accent you must be geordies - right?'

'Not far off the mark bonny lass - we're Weardalers. We live in a village twenty odd mile from Newcastle. Except Alistair here. He's from your neck o' the woods. He lives in Leeds.'

'Which part?' asked Katy.

'Bramley,' replied Alistair.

'Not far from us then.'

'Where's that then?'

'Pudsey. Well, me an' our Laura are. Elisa's from Manchester but she stays over a lot.'

'Whoa . . . ar divent nar if we should be speaking wi' you,' grinned Billy at Elisa. 'Newcastle's arch rivals yer see. We hate Manchester United. Do yer follow them?'

'Me? No. I've no interest in football,' replied Elisa.

'That's alreet then.'

'How aboot ye two?' asked Stuart of the sisters. 'Do you support Leeds United?'

'Not now. We used to do when we were younger. I hear they're not doing very well lately,' said Laura.

'Our Laura only follwed 'em years ago cos she fancied Gary Speed. Me dad sent him a letter an' he sent back a signed photograph for her birthday,' Katy informed them.

'That was over ten years ago!' retorted Laura. 'I couldn't fancy him now. Funny how your taste in men change as you get older.'

'Looking at that ring on yer finger, I assume yer've found someone yer more than fancy,' said Roy spotting a sizeable diamond solitaire on Laura's finger.

'True. I am engaged to be married.'

'Have yer set a date yet?'

'We certainly have. On the 1st of August when I marry Mark I'll be known as Laura Davis,' she said stretching out her hand, proudly looking at her engagement ring.

'Whey congratulations.'

'Aye, all the best fer the future,' added Billy.

'Thanks,' smiled Laura.

'Ar'll expect an invitation in the post then,' teased Roy before asking the other two girls, 'How aboot ye two then? Married? Single? On the look out?'

'We're both spoken for an' all,' replied Elisa.

'Four pint o' lager is it lads?' said Billy getting to his feet. 'Can I get you young ladies a drink?'

The girls looked at each other for a decision.

'We'd better not, but thanks,' said Laura. 'We're meeting up with some work colleagues shortly.'

'Whey, yer've time fer a quick half o' lager. I insist,' said Billy. 'Give us a hand at the bar Alistair.'

'I feel awful taking a drink an' then rushing off,' said Katy.

'Rubbish!' said Roy. 'It's nee problem bonny lass. Besides, you're lucky. It's not often Billy puts his hand in his pocket.'

Billy carried a tray of four pints, while Alistair placed a tray with three halves of lager on the girls table.

'Did yer need a hand wi' that heavy tray Ali?' teased Roy.

'At least I got off my backside to help,' came Alistair's retort.

'Now now boys, don't be falling out on yer day trip,' admonished Laura.

'Tek nee notice pet. It's normal behaviour between these two. They might be cousins, but they're definitely not kissing cousins - whatever that means,' said Stuart.

The girls thanked Billy for the drink.

'You're welcome ladies.' Billy raised his glass, 'Here's to the future.'

'Don't take offence but we're gonna be shooting off in a couple of minutes,' Elisa reminded Billy.

'Ar'd never dee that bonny lass. It's just a pity we didn't 'ave more time to get acquainted.'

'Yeah, it's a shame,' said Katy. 'I'm enjoying meself.'

'Where yer heading then girls?' asked Roy. 'Is it a pubbing an' clubbing neet?'

'It certainly is,' confirmed Laura. 'Yer've got to let yer hair down at the weekend. Forget the week completely and go for it.'

'My sentiments exactly,' agreed Roy, reaching across the table for his pint and involuntarily breaking wind. 'Oops! Excuse me!' he apologised with little humility. 'That was unintentional, ar can assure you.'

'Think nothing of it, we all do it,' said Katy, trying to supress a giggle, but only succeeding in setting the other girls off. 'We're used to it. Elisa farts for England in our house. Me mother bought an extractor fan for the living room, cos she's that bad.'

'Don't lie!' blushed Elisa. 'It's not true. Take no notice.'

'But it is true Elisa,' insisted Katy.

'I'll kill you when we get out of here,' said Elisa through gritted teeth.

'Divent worry pet,' said Roy. 'Even the Queen drops one now an' again. She literally does fart fer England,' he grinned.

Elisa relaxed, her reddened face returning to its normal colour.

'He's a bit of a comic your Roy. I bet you love his company,' said Laura, a mischievous glint in her eye.

'Oh aye . . . He's a laugh a minute is Roy. 'As us in stitches all day long,' stated a sardonic Billy.

'From dawn till dusk,' added Stuart sarcastically.

'They're tekking the urine. Ignore 'em,' said Roy, before changing the subject. 'Ar's badly in need of sustenance. Where's the nearest tekkaway ladies?'

'Briggate's full of 'em,' Katy informed him. 'Depends what you want. There's Pizza Hut, a Burger King, there's two MacDonalds on Briggate - one of 'em's almost opposite here.'

'Say no more. That'll dee me.'

'Katy an' Elisa have a degree in takeaways. That's all they eat,' goaded Laura. 'Between the pair of them, they alone keep half a dozen takeaways in business. You wouldn't believe the amount of calendars they get given at Christmas. Trouble is - they're all in a foreign language. Chinese, Indian, Mexican, Italian . . . you name it.'

'You don't half exaggerate our lass,' bemoaned Katy.

'Yeah, but most of it is true,' admitted Elisa.

'Go on, tek Laura's side.'

'Mind you,' said Laura, 'they did boycott takeaways for a couple of weeks last year. That was after finding half a cockroach type insect in their curry.'

'We were just unlucky,' stated Katy 'because that takeaway is really clean and hygenic.'

'It sounds it,' sneered Stuart.

'No, it really is!' You can watch them preparing the food and cooking it. They couldn't apologise enough when we told them about it.'

'They gave us our money back and offered us a free meal, but we declined the offer at the time because we didn't really fancy eating after that,' explained Elisa.

'Ar bet we've all eaten the odd insect without knowing it,' concurred Stuart.

'Aye, yer probably reet,' agreed Billy.

'Well, come on you two,' said Laura, finishing her drink. 'It's time to go.'

'Whey, it's been nice meeting you girls, even if it was only fer a short time,' said Stuart.

'Wait up, here's my business card,' said Roy, delving in his top jacket pocket.

Katy took it and read it out aloud, ' "Roy (the stud) Osborne. Anytime. Anyplace. Anywhere." The stud? Does that mean you inseminate horses then?'

'You shag horses?' chuckled Elisa.

'Arraway with yer! Yer set o' wind-up merchants,' Roy shouted after them as they left. 'Auf Wiedersehen Pets! And Elisa . . !'

'Yes?'

'Keep on farting fer England!'

'Shut up!' she replied bolting for the door and making a hasty exit.

'They were canny lasses,' remarked Stuart

'Aye,' agreed Billy. 'It's a pity they were all spoken for.'

'Why? Were yer ganna tek 'em back to Stanhope with yer?' mocked Roy.

'Do you 'ave to skit at everything we say?'

'Yep. That's my persona,' stated an unrepentant Roy.

173

'In fer a penny, in fer a pund,' declared Stuart getting up from his seat. 'Ar'll gan an' get us a short. Three rums an' a Baileys is it?'

'Yes please,' replied Alistair, fully aware that the question was aimed directly at him, Stuart already knowing what was Roy and Billy's chosen tipple. They always drank rum on these jollies. 'So, what do you think of Leeds then?'

'It's a reet shit-house,' declared Roy. 'Nar, I'm only kidding. Ar've not seen much of it, but what ar have, it's not bad.'

There was a momentarily pause.

'Is there summat up?' questioned Roy.

'No, I was just waiting for some derogatory remark to follow,' said Alistair.

'Ar divent nar, yer such a cynic Yorky.'

'I know I am - but with good reason.'

'He's here the lad,' announced Roy, watching as Stuart carefully place four shorts on the table.

They all took their drinks and the next minute was spent observing Roy rolling a bogey. Oblivious to the attention of the others, he wiped the offending bogey beneath the table top.

'You dirty git!' berated Stuart.

'What?'

'Divent act all innocent. We've been watching you this past minute.'

'Whatever turns you on.'

'Yer could try using a tissue,' suggested Stuart.

'Ar divent have any.'

'Try some bog roll then.'

'Give ower man, ar's keeping a cleaner in employment.'

'I doubt she'll clean under the top o' the table.'

'Whey, she should be sacked then.'

'Oh bollocks. I give up.' Stuart conceded defeat.

'Whey, it's getting canny busy now mind,' observed Billy.

'Most of them are passing through on a pub crawl,' said Alistair. 'They have one in each boozer an' finish off at a night club.'

'Lucky buggers. Nearest we get to a neet club back home is a lock-in in the Phoenix wi' the Darby an' Joan club,' bemoaned

Billy.

'Ar tell yer what bonny lads,' said Roy.

'What?' asked a facetious Stuart.

'These puffs an' lesbos . . . '

'Gays,' corrected Alistair.

'Whatever. These puffs an' lesbos divent give a toss aboot their sexual leanings . . . 'odding 'ands an' touching each other up in public. Could yer imagine 'em carrying on like that in a Stanhope boozer? They'd be driven out o' town man - Or at least put in in the stocks.'

'They're not doing owt illegal,' Alistair pointed out. 'An' stop exaggerating about 'em touching each other up an' all. Is it any wonder gays don't come out o' the closet in Stanhope? It's like living in the Stone Age up there. Yer've got yer fair share of bigots, that's for sure.'

'Well, ar tek as ar find,' stated Billy. 'As long as nee one bothers me, good luck to 'em.'

'Aye, me too,' added Stuart.

Alistair thought he'd stir the pot a little. 'It's said that someone who goes on about gays are actually inherent themselves.'

'Are you questioning my sexuality Yorky? I'm a ladies man through and through as well you nar.'

'I'll take your word for it.'

'Ha way an' sup up - I'm starving. Anyone want a burger? Ar's paying,' offered Roy, much to everyone's surprise.

'In that case, what we are waiting for?' said Billy, knocking back his rum.

'How come the spontaneous act of generosity?' asked Stuart. 'There must be a catch.'

'Do yer want a burger or not?

'Aye. Lead the way.'

The lads were seated on a bench outside McDonald's eating their burgers, barely tasting them as they watched the passers by, a large number of which were scantily clad young ladies.

'Ar could do this every week nee problem,' drooled Billy, his eyes in danger of popping out from their sockets.

'Skirts up their arses, thongs peeping out above their jeans . . .

175

We've died an' gone to erotic heaven,' lusted Roy. 'Ar daren't get up from this bench.'

'Yer've nee worries on that score hamster dick,' mocked Stuart. 'Stop deluding yer sen.'

'Shut it Milky. That's the last time I buy you a burger if that's the thanks I get.'

'Huh! What did it knock yer back? Seventy pence?

'It's the thought that counts.'

'An' don't think you're getting away wi' not buying a round of drinks just cos yer bought these burgers,' Alistair pointed out.

'Yer've probably been counting every round. That's typical of a Yorkshireman,' said Roy scathingly.

'Where's the nearest pub then Alistair?' asked Billy, throwing his burger wrapper into the bin.

'Just round the corner there, on the Headrow. Horse and Trumpet. The Vine's only about a hundred yards further down.'

'Is it full of totty then, this Horse and Trumpet?' asked Roy.

'I've no idea.'

'Never mind the totty. If it sells booze, it's good enough fer me,' stated Billy.

'Yer not interested in totty?'

'Roy! I'm interested in getting blathered. Let's be realistic here - Yer hardly ganna pick up a bird an' get a quick knee-trembler round the back o' the pub.'

'Yer never nar,' claimed the ever optimistic Roy. 'In fact, I'd put money on it.'

'You need to be staying overnight, visiting all the trendy wine bars an' pubs to have any chance of copping off,' Alistair told them.

'Now yer tell us Yorky.

'An' there's no point in going to them tonight, when we're leaving at ten o'clock.'

'Whey, it's all academic. Let's get to the pub,' said Billy impatiently.

'Yeah, ha way lads,' added Stuart.

'It's a bit of a pokey hole in here,' chuntered Roy, on entering the

Horse and Trumpet.

'Stop stalling fer time an' get to the bar,' said Stuart, giving him a shove.

'Alright, hold yer horses, ar's ganning.'

Alistair coughed as they made their way through the thick smoke to the bar.

'What's it to be then?' asked Roy. 'Shorts or lager?'

'Both,' said Billy.

'It's a tale. One or t'other. Mek yer mind up.'

'Shorts then lads?' suggested Stuart. 'We divent want to hanging in here longer than we 'ave to - it's an old man's pub.'

They all nodded their agreement.

'Are we going straight to the Vine then from here?' asked Alistair.

'We might as well if it's as near as you say it is Ali,' said Billy.

'Yeah, it's only a couple of minutes.'

'We'll gan straight there then. We'll go an' wind up the old Stanhope massive,' smirked Roy.

Walking down the Headrow, Stuart bent over to remove something sticking to the toe of his shoe. Roy quickly bent over him and to the amusement of the others, he simulated a back-scuttle. 'Gan on yer bitch! Squeal yer bastard!'

'Yer bleeding mental you!' shouted Stuart, struggling to escape Roy. 'Yer off yer rocker!'

Roy let go, laughing like a demented hyena.

'Whatever you do Roy, don't do a mooney,' advised Alistair. 'There's cameras everywhere. Drop a bit of litter or a cigarette butt an' yer'll be fined fifty quid. Now you go an' mug somebody, that's alright. They ignore robbery an' violence - it costs money to investigate.'

'Whey, nee bugger'll rob us - unless they're totally stupid,' said Roy. 'Mind you - we are in Yorkshire.'

'Watch it,' threatened Alistair.

'As yer nar Yorky, I'm no stranger to the martial arts,' boasted Roy.

'No stranger to bullshit, more like,' scoffed Stuart.

'You may mock, but yer winna be saying that when ar's fighting off half a dozen morons to keep you from injury. Having said that, you'd be off down the road like a whippet wi' diarrhoea first sign of any trouble. Orh . . . Bollocks! Ar've stood in some bleeding dog shite!' Roy's raised voice alerted the attention of two special constables crossing the Headrow. 'Give us some tissue Alistair, an' divent deny 'aving any, cos you always carry some fer when you jerk one off in the bog.'

'Right. Get yer own tissue,' came Alistair's response.

'Everything alright sir?' inquired one of the constables.

'Nar. Ar've just stood in some dog muck. It'll be one o' them beggar's dogs yer see tied to a piece o' string. They only use 'em fer public sympathy. Yer could check the surveillance cameras or tek a sample fer DNA if yer like. Mind you, it'd be nee good dragging a dog down to a cash point - they're notorious fer forgetting their pin numbers.'

'Very witty sir. Here's some Kleenex. Wipe your shoes, then use the bin,' instructed the second special.

'Will do officer. Thanks a lot.'

The lads had gone on ahead and were observing Roy's antics with much mirth.

'Yer could 'ave waited fer me yer set o' pillocks,' carped Roy.

'We were worried yer mouth'd get us locked up,' said Billy.

'Divent talk so soft man! They were very helpful as it turned out. Even gave me some tissue to wipe off the dog shite. They reckon it's a slim chance of apprehending the guilty dog though!'

'Yer daft bugger.'

'Here we are lads - The Vine. Whose shout is it?' questioned Alistair.

'Mine ar think,' said Stuart.

On entering the pub they were greeted by the raucous cheers of the Weardale clan, clearly the worse for wear but in high spirits.

Arthur called Alistair over. 'D'yer not remember leaving summat back at the Whitelocks?' he quizzed, before indicating the holdall on the seat beside him.

'Orh . . . thanks grandad. It's the booze. It makes me forgetful.'

'Never mind son. At least no one walked off with it.'

'Yeah. Thank God.'

'Lager or Baileys Alistair?' asked Stuart.

'A pint of lager please Stuart. Your friend gone home then grandad?'

'Aye. We swopped phone numbers. I said I'd give him a ring next time I was down so we can meet up again fer a drink. He's a canny fellow like. We had a great ol' chin-wag mostly aboot Leeds United. You 'ad a good time lad?'

'Aye, not bad grandad. We went for a drink in the Ship and got talking to three lasses from Pudsey. Nice girls. They didn't even tek offence to our Roy. That's got to be a first.'

'Ar nar what yer mean lad. He means no harm, but yer divent nar what he's ganna come out wi' next.'

Old Tom, sitting in the corner was trying his utmost to stay awake. Alf nudged him. 'We'll be off soon, yer can get yer heed down on the bus then.'

'I'm alreet Alf man. Ar could carry on drinking all neet,' bluffed Tom.

'I nar that,' patronized Alf. 'Ar wouldn't mind getting my heed down to be honest. Ar think it's this city pollution we've been breathing in all day. It meks yer lethargic.'

'Aye that'll be it,' agreed Tom.

Billy bought a last round of shorts for the lads.

'Mek that yer last drink, we'll be mekking tracks shortly,' said Joseph sipping his umpteenth orange juice.

Roy pleaded for an hours extension of the ten o'clock departure, but Joseph gave him short shrift. He couldn't wait to hit the road and get back home. A man could only drink so much coffee and orange juice in one day.

After a final visit to the gents, the Weardale clan set off for the minibus. Some walking steadily, some staggering, the progress was slow but sure. Frank offered old Tom a piggy-back but he stubbornly declined.

'I was talking to the landlady in the Vine,' said Roy.

'Big deal,' scoffed Stuart.

'Let me finish Milky - Anyway, she was telling me that she keeps reptiles but two of her chameleons died recently. She couldn't bear to part with 'em so her husband had her a pair of gloves made out of 'em. Trouble is - she can't find 'em!'

'Give me strength Lord,' uttered Joseph, looking to the heavens.

'Ar've got a million,' enthused Roy.

'Let's hope yer fall asleep sharpish then.'

Joseph eventually got his wish after enduring twenty minutes of Roy's lousy jokes and appalling out-of-tune singing. But once Roy had nodded off, the silence was utter bliss.

Getting away on time. No major incidents. No traffic hold-ups. Joseph was a happy bunny.

Any comments on this contemporary
novel are welcome or to buy any of
A L Craig's novels please telephone
07905 047226 or 07941 350877
e-mail kjccraig@aol.com

Weardale Days 'Up The Square'

Up The Square

The Day Trip

Tell Laura I Love Her

Turned Out Nice Again

Send In The Clowns

£5.99 each

FREE P&P UK DELIVERY